CHICKENS FOR THE BACKYARD HOMESTEADER

THE ESSENTIAL GUIDE TO CHOOSING AND KEEPING HAPPY, HEALTHY HENS

CHICKENS FOR THE BACKYARD HOMESTEADER

THE ESSENTIAL GUIDE TO CHOOSING AND KEEPING HAPPY, HEALTHY HENS

Suzie Baldwin

Photography by Cristian Barnett

Illustrations by Becca Thorne

Contents

My now intimate relationship with chickens began five years ago, shortly after I had purchased my house in the country and started my own "homesteading." Little did I know how close we would become and how fond I would grow of them.

When my first chickens arrived, we housed them in temporary accommodation, which was an old shed/summer house cordoned off with wire. When I was home I would let them out during the day to roam the garden. The chickens became so tame they would wander over to the kitchen door to say hello – perhaps with ulterior motives in the snack department. At sundown I would call, and they would come running, following me right back into their hut. My friend Shirley and her dog Maisie often came to stay, and the chickens would also quite happily follow them around the garden with Maisie on a lead. Then came the foxes, and a more secure residence was built, which a friend called "Peckingham Palace."

I have had my current set of three lovely Light Sussex for two years now. They produce the best eggs in the world. The best I have tasted anyway; creamy and delectable. Far superior to store-bought eggs. People ask me how I cook my eggs, and I have to explain it is the eggs themselves that are unmatchable.

When working away from home I miss keeping my "scraps" of food that I put aside for the chickens; I hate waste. My sister Natasha had chickens before me on her farm in New York, and she swore that their preferred meal was pasta and salad.

Earlier this spring one of my chickens was ill. Some of her feathers were missing, and her comb was pale. I talked to my very knowledgeable friends at the farm where I bought my hens, and they advised putting vitamins in the water. This pink colored tonic worked! Two weeks later her comb was a vibrant red again. I called my mother in New York, prattling on about how happy it made me to have nursed our chickens back to health.

Take my word for it, you become involved and fascinated. Sometimes, with all the traveling I do, I wonder why I keep hens. However, the moment I get home I wander out into the garden to collect the newly-laid eggs. They are a pale brown color, but worth their weight in gold.

Enjoy. *Joely*

Joely Richardson's recent work includes The Girl with the Dragon Tattoo, Showtime's The Tudors, and FX's Nip/Tuck.

Why keep chickens?

Keeping chickens

When I started keeping chickens, more than twenty years ago, it was looked upon as an odd, even bizarre, thing to do, and I was regarded as madly eccentric! Today, thankfully, keeping chickens is increasingly popular, especially, though not only, among "backyard homesteaders" looking for some degree of self-sufficiency. (See *Backyard Homesteading: A Back-to-Basics Guide to Self-Sufficiency*, Creative Homeowner, 2012.)

Chickens, if kept properly, are rewarding – and addictive. Once you have had even one or two, it is difficult to live without them. Many people who have lost their girls through old age or a predator say it leaves a huge hole in their lives, so be warned.

There are a few things to consider before you buy your chickens for your backyard homestead:

- Are there any local regulations, by-laws, or clauses in the deeds of your property that restrict you from keeping poultry?
- Do you have the time and resources? Chickens are inexpensive to look after, but the setup cost can be relatively expensive, and they need protecting from predators. Also, you need to be able to spend time with your girls to benefit not just from their eggs but also their enchanting characters.
- Think about the noise. Chickens are relatively quiet, providing you have no roosters, and they are at their noisiest when telling everybody they have laid an egg.
- You will also need to provide a chicken sitter for your girls when you are away on holiday. You can normally persuade a neighbor or friend with the bribe of letting them keep the lovely fresh eggs.

If you grow your own vegetables, chickens do a fabulous job of not just fertilizing your garden but scratching up weeds and generally cleaning it for you. They can attract rodents, but if you keep them clean and are careful with their feed, you should be fine. If you are a passionate gardener and love your flowers, do not let the chickens near them – their idea of a garden and yours are totally different! I describe my girls as my walking flowers.

If you feel that chickens are too much of a responsibility for you or take too much time away from your other "backyard homesteading" chores such as vegetable gardening, keeping bees, and so on, why not share them,

RIGHT: A friend's thoroughly spoiled Lemon Mille Fleur Booted Bantam hen.

and the chores, with friends or neighbors? There will be plenty of eggs to go around, and you can spread the word about backyard homesteading and self-sufficiency.

In my experience, if you choose to keep chickens, your life will change for the better. They are great stress reducers and endlessly fascinating – you can watch them for hours. It's also great to come home and be greeted by energetic clucks after a hard day at work, plus many people find they make a new network of friends who are happy to offer help and advice and buy their eggs. In addition, chickens teach children responsibility and respect. They soon learn that if they look after their chickens well, they will reap the rewards in eggs, in the satisfaction of a job well done, and believe it or not, in the acquisition of business skills. I have known several children who have bought chickens and gone on to earn money selling their eggs.

My aim in this book is to give you, as a backyard homesteader or potential backyard homesteader, a thorough guide to chicken keeping, including the confidence to happily look after your charges and avoid common problems. As with all animals, there can be difficulties, but the way you set up and treat your girls from day one will determine how successful and enjoyable your experience is. Most chicken problems can be prevented, and the more information you have at hand before you start, the less stressful and scary it will be – both for you and your chickens. With sections on:

- What to look for before buying chickens
- Getting your chickens to go to bed on their first night in their new home
- Maximizing your egg yield
- Dealing with broody chickens
- Ensuring your chickens are happy, whatever the season
- Keeping them healthy
- What to do when they reach the end of their lives

This book will help everyone from the complete beginner to the more experienced chicken keeper to get the most enjoyment from their flock.

In my opinion, chickens are easier to keep than dogs – they don't need to be walked – and they fit in very well with most lifestyles. They will soon recognize your voice and come running when they hear you, and give you more than love – fresh eggs! With care, and by following helpful tips based on years of experience, you can have calm, manageable egg layers eating out of your hand.

Keeping chickens has changed my life. I have made many friends on the journey, both young and old, and had the pleasure of collecting fresh eggs, which is especially pleasurable on a cold day, when they make great hand warmers.

COURSES ON CHICKEN KEEPING

Some chicken and feed suppliers run courses, past students of which have told me are very beneficial. County Cooperative Extension programs also offer educational programs. And some cities have poultry clubs that meet regularly and offer classes. Classes can be both informative and hands on, which is great if you are a beginner. Also, you get the chance to meet like-minded people, which can lead to new friendships. Check the Internet to see whether there are any courses running near you. Having attended one, you will know whether chicken keeping really is for you or not.

RIGHT: A free snack of freshly picked blackberries being relished by my Buff Orpingtons.

LEFT: You can never spend too much time watching your girls.

FIVE REASONS TO KEEP CHICKENS

1 A supply of fresh eggs – every day. Most "fresh" eggs bought from a supermarket are 3 to 5 days old.

2 They are the very best way of instigating a sense of care and responsibility in children. Children also love to collect eggs, and doing so helps to connect them with the reality of how food is produced.

3 They are easy to look after and make a large contribution to the self sufficiency that backyard homesteaders look for. There is also a breed out there to suit everyone and almost all gardens.

4 For their entertainment value. Chickens are endlessly fascinating, and simply being near them gladdens the heart and lifts the spirits.

5 Composted chicken droppings are rich in nitrogen, phosphates, and potash, and are a great fertilizer for the garden. Don't, though, put them directly in your garden without composting because the high levels of nitrogen will scorch the plants. Chickens also love to eat slugs.

FIVE COMMONLY ASKED QUESTIONS

1 How many chickens do I need? Depending on the breed, a hen will lay up to 300 eggs a year, so almost one a day. (See pages 43–52 and page 105.) I would recommend a minimum of three birds together because any fewer will bicker and quarrel.

2 Do I need a rooster? No. Chickens like to have a rooster around, but it doesn't affect how they lay. If you live in a built-up area, it's probably kinder to your neighbors not to have one. Also, some city ordinances allow only female flocks.

3 Where should I buy my chickens from? Always buy from a reputable supplier who is willing to give advice freely and offer help.

4 How long do hens live? A happy, free-range hen can live for anywhere from five to ten years, depending on the breed.

5 Do I need permission to keep chickens? If you are keeping chickens just for family use or as a backyard homesteader, you are unlikely to encounter any restrictions in rural or rural/suburban areas, but it is always advisable to check local planning regulations. Otherwise, check local and town/city ordinances and homeowner association restrictions.

Housing, equipment, and feed

Housing and equipment

To set up your chickens you will need a coop, a run (though some ordinances restrict outside runs), feeders and waterers, bedding, feed, and mixed grit, plus a dustpan and brush, paint scraper, disinfectant, and gloves to keep everything clean. Also, a basket to collect your eggs in.

A lady once visited my farm wanting to purchase two hens for her kitchen. When I said, "You mean the garden," she replied, "No, I intend to keep them in a dog cage in the kitchen as I only want them for eggs." I declined to sell her any of my girls!

Types of hen houses

There is an abundance of chicken coops and coop plans for do-it-yourselfers on the market from which to choose. If a house is very cheap it usually means that it isn't built to last. You need to make sure that the wood has been treated and is of a decent thickness for insulation and to keep predators out. The locks and hinges need to be robust and of a good quality, as does the wire for the run. Ideally perches should be removable, as this makes them easier to clean. Nest boxes should be accessible for you to collect the eggs. A rule of thumb is one nest box for three hens. Decide whether you want a fixed coop or a movable one. If it is movable you will be able to rest the ground regularly, although this does leave unsightly, worn areas. Fixed or non-movable coops can be made predator-proof and customized for your needs.

You can also buy plastic houses that are well designed and apparently completely predator-proof. These have less chance of getting red mites because they have fewer crevices. If a plastic house does get mites it is very easy to get rid of them by hosing out the coop (though this will not kill them). However, red mites are not that big a problem in the U.S. More problematic are northern fowl mites, which live on the birds themselves. (See page 124.)

You can also pick up secondhand coops. People tend to progress from the small units to bigger ones as they find they enjoy chicken keeping and decide to increase their flock. The small plastic houses make interacting with your girls rather difficult because you have to do everything on your knees.

I am definitely a wooden coop girl. I find them more natural and aesthetically pleasing.

RIGHT: Hybrid hens looking unsure in their new home.

HOUSE CHECKLIST

Timber: Make sure this is properly treated, so it will last and withstand the weather.

Roof: Choose wood or asphalt shingles, with an overhang for shedding water. You may also be able to find a corrugated roof, which will give better ventilation, made from waterproof fiberglass.

Ventilation: Holes covered with mesh will provide fresh air without drafts – the number required will depend on the size of the coop.

Pop holes: The entrance for the chickens is normally 1 square foot, usually with a sliding shutter or drop-down ramp with secure fastenings to keep out predators.

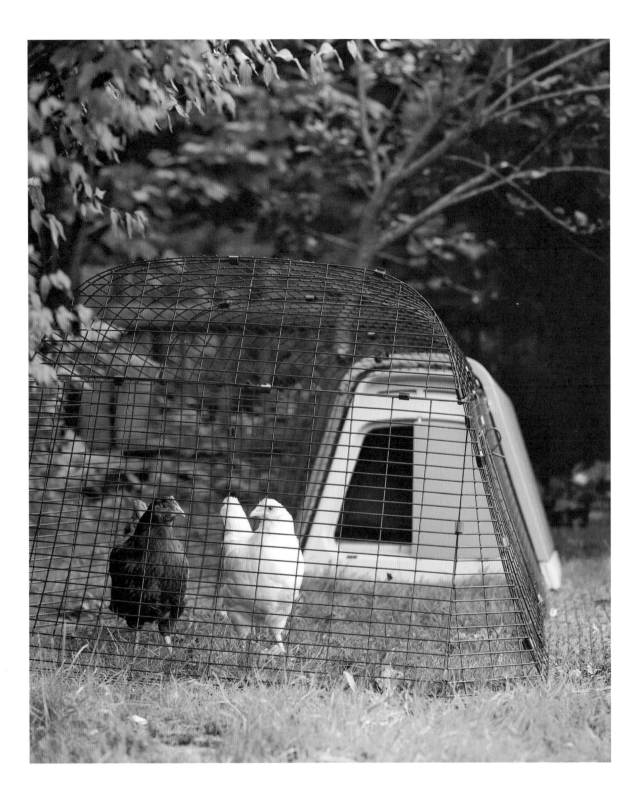

My favorite type of coop is a raised one with a raised run. It is easy to clean as it's at waist height; it provides a sheltered area underneath the coop to hang goodies, feeders, and waterers; and it deters rodents as there are no dark areas at ground level for them to rest in. The height of the run makes it feel airy and bright, even with shade on the roof; it lends well to having extension runs made easily; and it provides different levels for the chickens to be in. It can usually be moved by two people but can also be used in a permanent position.

How much space do you need?

There are no minimum requirements in the U.S., but many local ordinances have specific requirements, so you need to check local restrictions. Common recommendations are 0.75 square feet per pound of bird for indoor space and 3 to 4 square feet per bird for outdoor runs. However, I cannot emphasize enough that the more outdoor space you give them, the happier they will be.

Before buying your house and run, it is a good idea to think it through thoroughly. Spend time checking out all of the options; visit places that sell them; and have a look around, ask questions, and think outside the box! A customer came to see me and explained that she lives by a canal and has frequently seen a canal boat passing by with a chicken coop and run on the top. She felt that if you can keep chickens on a canal boat, she could certainly keep them in her garden.

Most gardens are suitable for chickens as long as you are sensible and do not keep too many. If you have a lot of hens in an inadequate space, you are asking for trouble. Not only will you have to clean constantly, but you'll have a constant battle with bad behavior and disease.

If you are on a budget, you can often buy secondhand coops, but make sure you check them over properly before buying. You can also convert sheds or old playhouses, provided they have ventilation and space for perches and nest boxes. Ventilation can be made by drilling some holes above the door and covering them with wire to prevent predators from getting in. Perches can be installed and nest boxes made very easily.

Lots of people come to my farm with pictures and videos of their coops and enclosures. Some are amazing - one couple had converted their summer house, and it had double glazing and central heating — and its own mailbox!

I have seen coops that have been painted to match the owners' house, teriffic coops made of armoires, wooden packing boxes, even a bathtub. Bearing in mind a chicken's requirements, let your imagination go wild.

Perches: These should be removable for cleaning, with a width of about 1½ inches and rounded for comfort. They should be placed higher than and away from the nest boxes. If you have more than one perch, they should be arranged so that the birds are not directly below each other.

Next boxes: The rule of thumb is one box for every three or four hens, but a minimum of two available. Place them low in the darkest part of the house.

Flooring: There is a choice of removable/slide out, fixed, slatted, or wired.

Runs: These should be as big as the space allows, made with good-quality wire, a wire roof, and base wire buried in the ground or firmly secured..

TOP LEFT: A fully enclosed, walk-in chicken coop. TOP RIGHT: Collecting eggs. BOTTOM LEFT: Treats are always welcome.

PROTECTION FROM THE ELEMENTS

LEFT: Shade is a must in very hot weather and can be as simple as adding an umbrella.

Partial shade is essential – if the chickens are in full sun all day, they can suffer from heat stroke. Shade can be provided by trees or shrubs, or a cover attached to one end of the run. Even a sun umbrella will work, and it can look really pretty.

Chickens need to be kept in a dry, draft-free location. Place the coop in a protected area near a wall or hedge, which act as windbreakers. It is also very important to choose a well-drained area for the run because chickens don't like being covered in mud, and puddles can breed disease.

BUILDING YOUR OWN HEN HOUSE

Building your own coop is likely to save more than half the cost of a ready-made one, so it may be something you want to consider doing if money is an issue. The easiest type to build is an ark, which has a nesting space at one end and a run at the other, although a straightforward, rectangular hen house is almost as simple. The Internet is a good source of ideas and information, plus plans, but make sure that whatever you build is large and comfortable enough for your chickens to rest at night and to extend their wings during the day. You also need to ensure that, in addition to a private and secure nesting area, your coop has a predator-proof run, easy access for cleaning, and a way of letting your chickens in and out easily.

Runs

It is easier and cheaper to buy unless you are very handy. I make mine using fence posts (6-foot finished height), which are buried in the ground, and attaching chicken wire with an overlap at both the top and bottom.The overlap at the bottom is important because it stops predators from digging underneath. It needs to be buried or secured with large tent stakes, concrete slabs, or large logs. Logs provide a habitat for bugs and frogs, but if you use too many, they'll also attract mice and rats. You only need a few to keep the wire firmly down. The overhang at the top is to prevent the predators from climbing in, as it will wobble and make him fall off.

I have also used barbed wire all the way around the posts, both at the top and again about 6 inches above the ground, but this is not a good idea if you have children. My sister managed to obtain some galvanized screens used on building sites, which work really well, but you do have to put a roof on top. She used plastic corrugated sheets, which you can get from most home centers. The bottom also needs securing with either wire or concrete slabs to prevent anything from digging in. Ground-level coops are good in small gardens because they are easy to move around, but they are vulnerable from predators around the bottom.

Chickens love to dust-bathe. It keeps them healthy, cleaning their feathers, removing excess oil, and suffocating any mites that might be living on them. If they have a dry, sheltered area in their run with dirt in it, they will make their own. If they are out every day in your garden, they will soon find a favorite spot to dust-bathe, usually in a sheltered position under a bush, away from predators, so they can relax. If they have none of the above, you can provide them with a dust bathe very easily; all you need is a high-sided container – large seed trays filled with dry soil, sand ash, or peat moss work well. You can also add mite powder to their dry dust bath for both cleaning and prevention.

ABOVE: An overhang of chicken wire with barbed wire helps keep out predators. RIGHT: Houses can benefit from being in a sheltered area during the winter months.

Pop holes

I have never used automatic pop holes because I'm a great believer in having contact with your chickens, and these make it all too easy for you to not see them. Watching the chickens as you let them out in the morning and put them to bed is the perfect time to check on them. Having kept chickens for so long, I am also well aware that occasionally, particularly on beatiful summer nights, the girls will wander around the house rather than go inside. If you use an automatic closing device, it is so easy for one or two to be locked out for the night because it works by sensing light and is incapable of counting your chickens in. A lot of my customers love these devices, and I have heard many great reports about them. However, I cannot advocate their use.

Rats dislike the smell of mint, so if you have a problem with them, try growing some near your run to deter them.

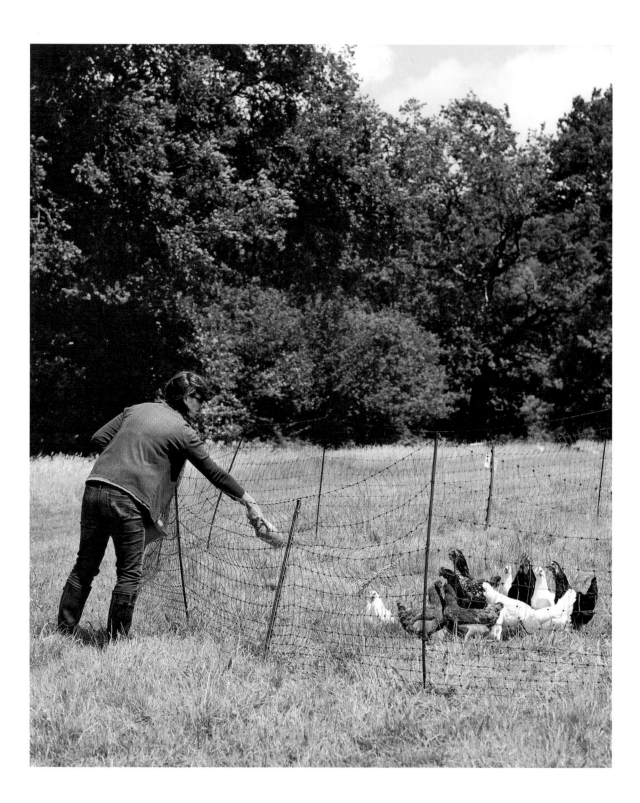

ELECTRIC FENCING

LEFT: My girls free-ranging in an electric fence enjoying a daily scratch of corn.

Electric fencing is a very good way of keeping your girls safe if used correctly. It is a flexible option, as it is easily moved, allowing you to utilize different areas of your garden. But it does require maintenance, regular cutting of the grass around the fence, and checking with a tester daily to ensure that it is working. Some units have alarms that let you know when the power is low. I have used electric fencing for many years with great success, except for this year when a determined fox jumped in. Unfortunately, once a fox has found a way in, he will return, which meant that I had to move my remaining chickens to a permanent fixed enclosure while I dealt with him. Since dealing with him, I have had no further problems and am using the electric fencing again.

You do need to keep the power on for 24 hours a day because when it is off, it can be chewed by rodents, rabbits, and foxes, which will cause damage and affect the voltage.

The bottom strand of the fencing is not electrified, but all the others are, so if the grass or foliage is too high and touch the second line, it will "ground," or drain the power, making it less effective. Regular checking for any debris, such as fallen branches, is important because this can also ground the power. Frogs and toads can also get zapped and die on the wire. This will affect the power, so a regular walk around when you let the chickens out and put them to bed is advisable.

There are many units available. Some run on main power, which I prefer, but this does limit where you can use them. Batteries are available, and some chargers work off solar panels and can be very effective. Whatever kind of charger you choose, it is best to buy direct from the supplier because they are usually on hand to offer help and advice. If buying from a retailer, ask about what telephone support you can expect.

RIGHT: A Polish cock nesting in straw.

BEDDING

The bedding you choose really depends on the weather. In the warmer months, chunky sawdust is great, but it needs to have the actual dust extracted as chickens are susceptible to respiratory problems. Horse bedding works really well and is much larger than normal sawdust. Straw is good, but it tends to compact. In colder months, pine shavings are great because they also insulate the coop. Avoid using them, however, in the warmer months, as your hens do not need the added warmth. Newspaper can be used, but be aware that some chickens use it as a toy. I once purchased two new layer houses that could take 50 chickens each and meticulously lined them with newspaper with a small amount of shavings on top. The girls loved it, but when I returned to check on them later, they had removed the sheets of newspaper and were running around the field with them. The mess was horrendous, but they were having a great time! Never use hay. It can be eaten by the chickens and form a tight ball in their gizzard, causing problems such as gizzard impaction. (See page 130.)

ENTERTAINING YOUR CHICKENS

RIGHT: Scarecrows are easy to make and can deter predators, as can a radio left playing.

During the hot, dry months of summer, my family and I spend a lot of time with our chickens. They wander around the garden scratching and bathing while we attend to the vegetable patch or flower beds, and there are plenty of bugs for them to chase. Life is great! It all changes as the nights get darker and the days colder. We tend not to be in the garden as much, so the chickens spend more time confined to the run. This is when your chickens could do with some entertainment. I don't mean a television set, although on occasions I have been known to turn on a radio for them in the run. This provides different sounds that predators don't like, and the hens seem happy. Hanging old CDs gives them something different to look at. A perch hung like a swing provides hours of amusement. Old logs for them to jump on and peck at are good, too. You can fill the clear balls that have toys in them (the type you get from vending machines in supermarkets) with mealworms and make some holes in them, so that when the chickens peck and push them around, the mealworms drop out. This is much more fun than just throwing the mealworms on the floor.

Chickens are very inquisitive and enjoy variety in their surroundings, so try different things, and experiment – just make sure whatever you use is safe, with no sharp edges or small pieces that the chickens would be able to swallow. I enjoyed making a scarecrow, which sat on a chair in the run. It didn't take the girls long to sit on its knee and explore it, and was something to make predators wary!

Feed

FEED

Feeding chickens is very easy nowadays; there is a huge choice of ready-made complete food on the market. Which kind you choose is entirely up to you, but try to buy food that is as natural as possible and GM (genetically modified) free. Some feed has colorants added, which make the egg yolks bright yellow.

Chicks from day one to about 6 to 8 weeks need starter cumble. They then need grower or pullet developer until they're 18 weeks old, and from then for the rest of their lives they need layer's crumble, pellets, or mash. Layer's crumble looks like Grape Nuts cereal and is easier for the birds to eat; pellets are pressed into small, cylinder-shaped pieces. Mash has the same ingredients but is a fine dust, which makes eating more time consuming for the chickens. This is seen as a benefit by some poultry keepers because it can help to occupy the chickens, giving them less time to become bored. However, I always feed my girls crumble or pellets. I find them cleaner and less wasteful. Chickens will waste a certain quantity of the mash, and I find that it becomes damp and clogs feeders as it draws moisture from the air.

Whatever you choose, it is always advisable when changing the feed to do it gradually, mixing half and half for a week or so until the chickens slowly become used to it. I believe in feeding layer's pellets on an ad hoc basis, meaning that it is available to the girls all day long.

The feed requirement of your chickens will vary depending on the weather; in colder weather they will consume much more in order to keep warm.

Never mix layer's pellets and corn together. Mixed corn is like chocolate to chickens and they will favor this over the layer's crumble or pellets, which contain the most goodness. But it is a great afternoon treat for them, best given by throwing a small handful of the corn into the run, allowing the chickens to scratch and forage for it.

WHERE TO STORE YOUR FEED

Most chicken feed – layer's crumble or pellets, mash, and mixed corn – comes in 50-pund bags. It is the cheapest way to buy your feed but needs to be stored in a cool, dry, ventilated place to prevent it from going moldy. You should not store it directly on the floor. Raise it using a wooden pallet or something similar. It is important not to encourage any predatory local

---

WHAT TO FEED YOUR CHICKENS

This varies depending on the age of your chickens, as follows:

Hatch to 6–8 weeks: Starter crumble
6 to 18 weeks: Grower or pullet developer
18 weeks on: Layer's crumble (or pellets) or mash

When changing feed, do it gradually, mixing half and half for a week until your chickens become used to it.

TOP LEFT: Layer's pellets provide everything a girl could need. TOP RIGHT: Dandelions are loved by chickens. BOTTOM LEFT: Dock leaves are great to hang as a treat. BOTTOM RIGHT: Mixed grain or corn is a great afternoon treat but should be used in moderation because it tends to dilute the diet and make birds fat.

wildlife, so storage bins, either metal canisters or plastic boxes with lids, work well. If you're using plastic, be aware that vermin can chew through it, but not usually overnight, so check every day. If you see any signs, take appropriate action.

Remember that the bags of food you buy have a *best before* date. Although the food will look fine after this date, using it means that the nutrients and vitamins will have depleted. Most feed seems to have a shelf life of 3 months.

In the past, farmers fed their chickens greens because they believed it increased the size of their eggs.

CHICKENS' FIVE-A-DAY

Chickens benefit from having a daily portion of green vegetables because they contain minerals. This is the equivalent of our five-a-day, and helps the chickens' digestive system to function well. Raw is best, and it is advantageous to hang the greens so that the girls can peck at them more naturally. But too much cabbage and broccoli can cause diarrhea, so just give a little of this.

Although lettuce has very little nutritional value, it is great at keeping a hen's digestive system working well. It is also easy to grow yourself. Onions also aid digestion and can help ward off many illnesses, but don't give them too many because onions make eggs taste odd. Potato skins/peelings should be blanched before feeding. They love these in the winter months mixed with bran. Nettles are very good for them — and free. Collect them when they are young; cut them up; boil them; and add to their layer's crumble, or alternatively just hang them in bunches. Don't forget to wear gloves.

Other treats your chickens will enjoy include blackberries, dandelions, dock leaves, and chickweed, to name just a few. Always remove any uneaten food, and discard it at the end of every day.

FEEDERS

There are many feeders on the market:

• **Treadle feeders** work by means of a paddle that the chicken steps on to open it. They are very good and prevent rodents being able to eat any food, but you will need to train your chickens to use them.

• **Outdoor galvanized feeders** are robust and look attractive. They really need to be placed on a brick or level log because they are rather low for the girls if put on the floor.

• **Trough feeders** are quite wasteful because the chickens can scratch at them and contaminate the feed by defecating in them.

• **Plastic feeders** that can be hung up are by far my favorite. You can hang them so that the lip is at the birds' back height to prevent waste. This prevents the birds from scratching the food out of the feeder and from scratching mud and dirt into it. They are easy to fill, and the food never becomes stale because it naturally filters out. They are also easy to clean.

Whichever style you choose, you need to make sure you have sufficient space around the feeders for all of the chickens to be able to feed at the same time.

WATERERS

Chickens drink a lot and enjoy fresh, cool water. There are a lot of waterers to choose from – the size you need will depend on how many chickens you are keeping.

• **Bucket fountains** look great and are easy to use. They are galvanized buckets with half a lid. You just fill as normal, and lay them on their side.

• **Jam jar waterers** are easy to fill and use, and they can be hung up. They are old-fashioned and, being made of glass, look attractive, but you need to be aware that they will break when dropped.

• **Plastic waterers** aren't as pretty as glass ones but are robust and easy to use and clean.

• **Nipple waterers** are hygienic and easy to set up, and have the advantage of keeping the chickens busy.

Remember that many things can be used to hold water, but they need to be kept clean and hygienic. You don't want the poor girls climbing into them, and you ideally want mud and dirt kept out. I've even seen discarded gallon milk containers used; they are actually effective — and free. Remember, too, that waterers should be placed in the run and never in the house, because a damp bedding area is not healthy for the chickens.

MIXED GRIT

Mixed grit, which contains flint and oyster shell, is an essential part of a chicken's diet. Because chickens have no teeth, the flint is used to help grind the food in the gizzard. The oyster shell is a source of calcium and helps produce strong egg shells. There are grit stations on the market. They work well, but if you have a small run they can take up precious space. I find throwing a small handful of grit into the run regularly is fine. It encourages the chickens to forage naturally and doesn't clutter the run with another feeder. Grit doesn't attract pests, so you don't have to worry about that.

TOP LEFT: A selection of waterers. TOP RIGHT: A galvanized bucket waterer. BOTTOM: A selection of feeders.

TREATS

Everybody deserves a treat occasionally, and chickens are no exception. You will get as much enjoyment from watching as they will get from eating them. Bake some cookies, but leave out the sugar and chocolate chips and add peanuts or raisins instead. Thread them on string, and hang them up for the chickens to peck at. Fallen leaves collected and placed in a big pile will make them go crazy. Cereals threaded on to string and hung in the run provides them with hours of activity.

A child-size soccer ball placed in the run will be investigated for quite a while, and a treat ball that you can get from pet shops, filled with mealworms, will be pushed around for hours. And corn on the cob hung up for them will make them jump for joy! Logs with holes randomly drilled in and stuffed with rice or peanut butter causes great excitement.

Old baby toys, rattles, and hanging mirrors will make the chickens very inquisitive. Baby gyms are great; the birds also use them as perches. Make fat balls for them filled with mealworms, sunflower seeds, stale bread crumbs, and the like. Grow sunflowers, and collect their seeds in the summer to use as winter treats – they will help the girls' feathers to grow.

Chilled watermelons are very refreshing and help keep chickens

TOP LEFT: Home-grown corn on the cob provides great entertainment when hung up. TOP RIGHT: Apples hung in a bird feeder. BOTTOM LEFT: O-Shaped cereal threaded on string provides hours of fun. BOTTOM RIGHT: Sunflower seeds are a delicious treat.

Chickens are omnivores; they eat both vegetables and meat.

hydrated in the summer. Grapes (seedless) are loved if just thrown into the run. This is entertaining to watch as the girls get protective of their find. You can buy live crickets from pet shops to give them, which makes a great game, and the insects are packed with protein.

Use bird feeders stuffed with vegetables or fruit to make life a little more interesting. Threading cooked pasta onto string for the hens is something my children love to do and is always relished. Chickens also enjoy frozen bananas (as do my children). Freeze berries with natural yogurt in ice-cube containers for a fantastic summer treat. Also hang a full yogurt container, with a hole cut in the bottom, so the yogurt drips out. Natural yogurt is very good for the chickens' digestive system.

Do not feed treats that are high in sugar or salt, and always cook potato skins. Raw or undercooked beans are poisonous, as are avocados, which contain a fungicidal toxin called persin that has been known to cause cardiac distress and heart failure. Raw egg should never be given because it can encourage the girls to egg eating. All chickens have different likes and dislikes, so see what works for yours.

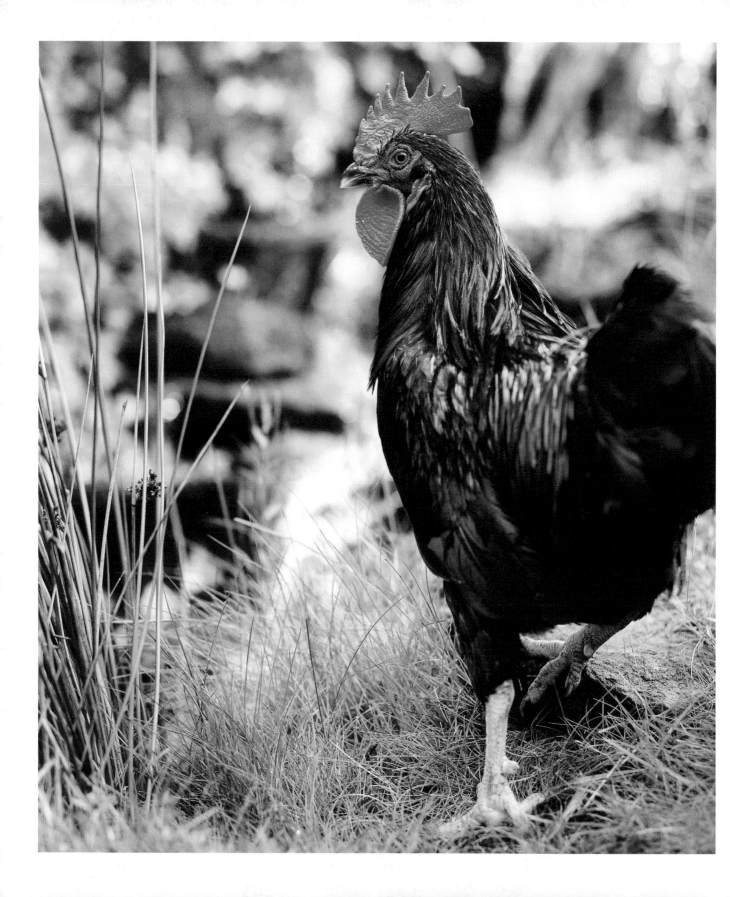

Choosing your chickens and getting them home

Choosing your chickens

TOP LEFT: The Rhode Island hybrid is a popular choice to start with.
TOP RIGHT: A hybrid utility Light Sussex is a fanastic layer.
BOTTOM LEFT: Hybrid White Leghorns lay pure white eggs.
BOTTOM RIGHT: The hybrid black sex-link is a stunning bird.

I have kept many other breeds, but the ones I have mentioned here hold a special place in my heart. Remember to do your research and speak to other poultry keepers before deciding on what's right for you. We all have different likes and dislikes, so what's right for me might not be best for you.

Utility breeds are reared for eggs and, when they become less productive, you can eat them. Orpington, Brahma, Rhode Island Red, Plymouth Rock, Jersey Giant, Faverolle, and Houdan are just a few examples of pure-breed utilities. I have eaten some of the cockerels I have raised that I didn't need to keep. I tend to use commercial meat birds, which you can buy very reasonably from commercial hatcheries. They grow fast and are hardy, and they taste fantastic, making them worthy of a place in the garden. If you wish to raise your birds for meat, the best tip I can give you is DO NOT NAME THEM! I am a real animal lover, but I am not vegetarian. I have a lot of comments from people who are horrified to find that I eat my own chickens. All I can say is that my girls and boys have a terrific free-range life, are treated with respect, and are thoroughly enjoyed. I can also hold my head up and say that I have no part in battery eggs or intensively raised meat. The first time you sit down to dinner to eat one of your own birds is hard, but the immense satisfaction of a job well done soon helps you to forget the not-so-nice part.

The best age to get your chickens is at point of lay – from 16–21 weeks – especially if you're a complete beginner. You can be certain that they're hens and not cockerels, and no special care or diet is needed. They usually start laying, depending on the season, at around 19–21 weeks. They are also still young enough to tame.

HYBRIDS

Hybrids are available worldwide and are chickens that have been bred by mixing different breeds together to produce one that excels at egg laying. They are very hardy, healthy birds. All brown egg layers are based on the Rhode Island Red. All white layers on the White Leghorn.

• **Black Sex-Link:** Stunning birds with a lovely iridescent sheen, these are happy as long as they are well fed.

• **Hybrid Ameraucanas:** These chickens are blue- and green-egg layers. They lay a medium-size egg and do well in backyard and range environments. They come in unique, assorted, and brilliant colors.

• **Hybrid Barred Rocks:** These chickens are common brown-egg-laying birds. They have barred, or striped, plumage.

• **Hybrid Reds, or Red Sex-Links:** are a popular choice to start with. They are very good layers – expect up to 300 eggs a year given the right food and housing conditions – and come in a variety of colors, from black to ginger, speckled blue and off-white. They all make lovely placid family pets. They will give you different colored eggs, ranging from pure white to dark brown and even blue. Hybrids from different suppliers are given different names.

• **White Leghorn:** A beautiful pure-white chicken with a larger-than-average comb, which flops over to one side like a bonnet. Somewhat nervous and better in a free-range environment, this utility bird reminds me very much of a slender ballerina. She lays pure white eggs.

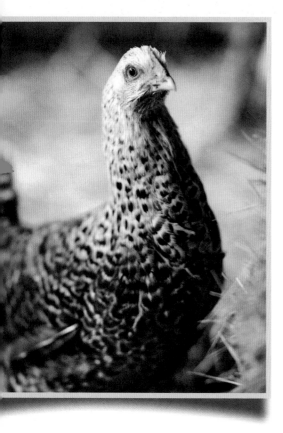

ABOVE: A Barred Cross hen.
RIGHT: A Bearded Buff Laced Polish cockerel.

PURE BREEDS

Pure breeds come in an abundance of shapes, sizes, colors, and personalities. They are classed as pure breeds because they breed true, meaning their young will always resemble their parents. All pure breeds have their own standards (what the breed is required to look like, i.e,. the shape, color, and size), which in the U.S. are sanctioned by the American Poultry Association (APA). The APA recognizes 350 different breeds and varieties of chickens. The following are pure breeds I have kept myself:

• **Araucanas** are renowned for laying blue eggs, but in fact they range in color from blue to green to pink! They are fun and have an upright gait and funny-looking ear tufts. They come in lots of colors, lavender being the most common. They adapt well to being confined and lay a very good amount of eggs. Having their eggs in your basket certainly causes a stir!

• **Barnevelders** lay lovely dark eggs, and lots of them. They are somewhat lazy, so you need to watch their diet because they can become fat. Being large, they can be kept with a low fence. (But remember, it won't keep out predators.) They are well suited to confinement and are remarkably hardy. I had a stunning group of penciled girls that were very easy to keep.

• **Brahmas** are my absolute favorite of the heavy meat breeds. They have feathery feet, amazing bottoms, and an expression that always makes me giggle. They are very calm and placid birds and make wonderful pets. Their egg size is rather disappointing considering their size, but they lay around 140 eggs a year. Brahmas do go broody and make lovely moms, but they have a tendency to tread on their eggs and break them, and can accidentally do this to their young too. Brahmas come in an array of colors. My trio of Brahmas have made many people gasp at their beauty. Brigadeir, my particularly gorgeous rooster, was a real head-turner as he marched through the yard, and being as large as a small child, he had a certain presence about him.

Pure breeds

Hard-feathered breeds are game birds with tight, short feathers that follow the shape of the body. They include Old English Game, Malay, Aseel, and Modern Game.

Heavy breeds have lovely temperaments. They were developed for both eggs and meat and tend to eat a lot. They include Brahma, Orpington, Dorking, Cochin, and Faverolle.

Light breeds are good egg layers but not table birds. They can be flighty and nervous. They include Araucana, Ancona, Hamburg, and Leghorn.

True Bantams are naturally small birds and are usually only kept to show or as pets. They are great if space is an issue. Examples are Cochin, Japanese, and Sebright.

Rare breeds are less common. They include Dominique, Andalusian, Houdan, Java, Redcap, and Sussex.

LEFT: A Mille Fleur Cochin hen looking very proud.

• **Campines** are beautiful birds and quite wild. They are not a breed to keep if you are short of space. They have a very unsettled personality, and even with patience they remain wild at heart – believe me, I have tried every trick and bribe I know. They do not make good broodies but lay an abundance of white eggs throughout the year.

• **Cochins** are very large with feathery feet and a lovely bottom! When you watch them pecking around, it looks as if they are wearing bloomers. These chickens are friendly, contented, and easy to keep. They need a mud-free run due to their feathery feet. The eggs they lay are small considering the size of the girls, and they lay about 115 eggs a year. They make lovely mothers. They come colored black, blue, buff, white, partridge, and mottled. Rocky was my star rooster who produced some fantastic offspring. He was a real gent until the spring came, when he turned into a nightmare, running at whoever entered his pen, launching himself at you spurs first. Because of his size and weight he could certainly pack a punch. These are dual-purpose birds, meaning they can be eaten as well as lay eggs. Their feathers are fantastic for stuffing cushions.

• **Faverolles** are very distinctive, with a lovely beard and muff, and they have five toes. They are fast-growing, with a friendly, tranquil nature, and they lay around 115 eggs a year. It is not unknown for my girls to lay into the winter. Because they are so friendly and polite, they can be bullied by more boisterous breeds. These are my favorites to watch because they are so serene and sedate, and you can almost feel the stress of the day slip away. You can eat them, and their meat has a lovely texture.

• **Leghorns:** I love these girls; they look like little ballerinas and are very agile and always on the go. They lay lots of large white eggs and come in many colors. They love to range freely and are quite capable of roosting in the trees. Their combs and wattles are large and sometimes need protection in very cold weather. The combs give the appearance of a lopsided bonnet balancing on a very petite head.

• **Marans** are prolific egg layers, and they lay beautiful chocolate-brown eggs. They are more flighty than the other heavy breeds mentioned but are friendly, busy girls that can be easily tamed. They come in a variety of colors, including cuckoo, black, and copper/black. They make good mothers and are intelligent and alert.

• **Orpingtons** are stunning and are often featured in magazines. They have lovely personalities and are calm and inquisitive. Because of their size, they are neither flighty nor escape artists; they need larger houses with low perches. Their feathers are gorgeous and soft. They come in black, blue, buff, and white. They tend to go broody and make lovely mothers. For a pure breed, their eggs are large, and they produce around 160 in a season; but because of their placid nature, they can be bullied by other breeds.

• **Polish** are lovely and have a huge ball of feathers on their heads (crests). They are very comical to watch, extremely good pets, and a reasonable layer of small white eggs. They need extra care because of their head feathers; they can be prone to eye infections and are best kept with their own kind. Their crest also impairs their vision, which makes them slow to react, so they are best kept in runs.

• **Welsummers** are traditional farmyard chickens that lay lovely dark brown eggs, and lots of them. They are hardy and spend a lot of time foraging. They don't go broody too often, but when they do, they make fabulous mothers. I had several Welsummers a few years ago, and they often used to trot into my sunroom to share my after-dinner desserts!

BANTAMS are the smallest chickens, and they are very popular when space is an issue. Examples are:

• **Japanese Bantams** are really elegant chickens with very upright tails and slightly drooping wings. Their legs are very short and can hardly be seen. They are not very good in the cold or in wet weather, as their chests can get very wet due to their tiny legs, so they are better suited to a sheltered area or being indoors. They make great, friendly pets, so are extremely well suited to small children. However, they are not very good egg layers at all.

• **Bantam Cochins** are my favorite small chickens. They walk like Charlie Chaplin and have personalities that would suit a lion. They need a dry run because their short, feathery feet can get very wet and muddy. They are hardy and robust, and mix well with most breeds if given enough space. They are good broodies and make very protective moms. Expect around 120 small-sized eggs a year, although this number really does depend on how much time they spend being broody. You will see Bantam Cochins in a vast array of colors.

ABOVE: A pair of purebred Japanese Bantam hens. OPPOSITE PAGE TOP LEFT: A Non-bearded Black Silkie hen makes an attractive sight in any garden. TOP RIGHT: A purebred Partridge Cochin hen. BOTTOM LEFT: A purebred Lemon Mille Fleur Booted Bantam hen. BOTTOM RIGHT: A Non-bearded White Silkie hen is a bird with a lot of character.

- **Sebrights** are compact chickens with fantastic tails, and the lacing on them is truly stunning, almost as if they have been painted. To see one close up is amazing. They are very likable and calm, but they do not lay many eggs.

- **Plymouth Rock Bantams** exhibit high egg production and a meaty body for small birds; better-than-average hardiness; hens that tend to broodiness and make good mothers; and a docile disposition. The breed was very popular in the U.S. in the late nineteenth century but went out of favor. Today that are making a comeback among backyard homesteaders.

- **Silkies:** I would never be without this breed in my garden. They are adorably fluffy and cute and such endearing characters. Gertrude, a truly adorable girl (if not a little headstrong), used to be a regular in my kitchen. Her mannerisms even made my husband smile as she demanded treats and argued with our Jack Russell dog over the water bowl. Gertrude was often spotted on the back of a patio chair surveying her land. She raised many broods in her time – even ducks.

  Their feathers are fluffy, more like fur, and because of this their feathers can get wet very quickly. They also have blue skin and flesh and a fifth toe. In my experience I have found Silkies to be hardy and easy to keep. They do, however, spend a great deal of time being broody, so do not expect many eggs, which come in many different colors.

The tyrannosaurus rex is a very distant relative of the chicken.

Where to buy your chickens

If you are a beginner, it is advisable to go to a reputable breeder to buy your chickens. You should look around the establishment and be able to view your chickens and their environment. They should offer you advice and answer your questions freely. In my view they should also question you if they care about their birds. I can spend up to an hour with beginners going through questions and reassuring not only myself but my customers that the chickens are right for them. Most good breeders will give help over the phone. I encourage people to update me on their chickens. Never buy chickens that you have not seen.

A lady who had purchased some hens from another breeder came to visit me. They had become ill very quickly, and when she phoned the breeder, he wanted nothing to do with them. It transpired that she had not seen the birds or their environment but had just accepted the box of chickens, which were very underweight, lethargic, and covered in lice. With lots of tender loving care and some antibiotics, wormer, and lice powder, they made a full recovery – but she has no idea what age they are or whether they have been vaccinated or not.

Another person who had originally bought his chickens from me phoned to say that they were all ill. The symptoms included a hunched appearance, being lethargic, sneezing, and not laying any eggs. After a while I discovered that he had bought two hens that didn't look quite right at a market, but he put it down to stress. He had put these in with my hens, and they all became ill with *mycoplasma gallisepticum*. (See page 123.)

Beware, there are lots of people out there jumping on the chicken-selling bandwagon to make easy money. Make sure you stick with established breeders, and go by word of mouth. Always check the chickens and their environment, and if you don't like the look of either, trust your instincts and walk away. I have been keeping chickens on a large scale for more than 5 years. It isn't easy, and it doesn't make you rich; it is a way of life and a passion. I like to look after my girls as I would look after my children, and when you have up to a thousand, it is a huge job.

DOS AND DON'TS

Do
- Handle and check the bird yourself
- Ask questions
- Look around
- Take your time
- Keep a minimum of three birds

Don't
- Buy a bird you have not seen and checked
- Buy one that you feel sorry for
- Buy if you are not happy with the way the chicken is being kept

RIGHT: A fabulous White Silkie cockerel.

TOP LEFT: Holding a chicken with her wings in. TOP RIGHT: A sure indication this girl has been pecked (note the V-shaped feathers left). BOTTOM LEFT: Comb of a Speckled Sussex. BOTTOM RIGHT: An inquisitive hybrid pullet.

WHAT TO LOOK FOR

Once you have chosen where you are going to get your chickens, here's what to look for when you check them. Don't feel silly, because a good breeder will be only too happy to accommodate you. I check over the chickens with all of my customers as a matter of course.

The chicken you choose should be quick and alert. Never pick a hunched-up, sleepy-looking one because you think she is docile! It usually means that she is sick. It's normal for a chicken to run away when you are trying to catch her – this is not a sign of her being unfriendly.

Once caught, she may make a fuss for a while (I would if I were caught and picked up!), but this is perfectly normal. Talk to her, and hold her comfortably. If you're not confident, just ask the breeder to show you how. Then look at her eyes – they should be bright and clear and should never have any discharge. Check her comb – if she is a young pullet (16 to 18 weeks old) it will be small and pink; if she is slightly older, it will be upright and red. Some breeds, such as the Blues, have a bluish tinge to their skin, and this is perfectly normal. Her beak should be a natural shape. There shouldn't be any discharge or smell coming from the nostrils. The legs should be smooth and clean. The feathers need to be clean and glossy, with no bald patches, and the bottom (vent) should also be clean.

You can tell whether a chicken is in lay or not by measuring the width between her pelvic bones. In a mature hen in full lay there should be a gap the width of about two three fingers.

EX-BATTERY HENS

You can now purchase ex-battery, or spent, hens (those at the end of their commercial life, which is usually 1 to 2 years) very cheaply. They will be lacking in feathers, not know how to perch, and be very nervous of the great outdoors. But in a short time and with plenty of love, patience, and good feed, they will re-feather and gain confidence. People find this very satisfying, but it can be emotionally draining and stressful if you are new to chicken keeping. You should know, however, that these hens will lay fewer and poorer-quality eggs because of their older age.

You can call a chicken a chicken regardless of its age or sex.

Getting them home

RIGHT: A traditional
movable chicken coop.

Before you go to collect your chickens, it is very important that their coop and run are ready for them. Ensure that the coop has sufficient bedding in it and that there is feed – preferably the one the chickens are used to – and cold water. If you haven't visited the place from which you are going to get your chickens (which I advise that you do), phone them beforehand to ask if they could let you have some feed to bring home with you. The chickens do not need the stress of moving *and* new food. Peel and slightly crush two cloves of garlic, and place them in the girls' water – this is great for a chicken's immunity, which will be lowered with the stress of moving. Picking up new chickens is always very exciting, but explain to any children coming with you the need to be quiet on the way home.

One memory I have is of a lovely family with three excitable children coming to pick up their chickens from me. All was going well until the father placed the box containing the three chickens on the knee of his eldest daughter in the car. This was greeted with hysterical screaming, and while arms were flailing, I managed to take the box out of the car. As the parents went about calming the situation, I firmly explained how the noise and behavior was unacceptable because the chickens would have been truly traumatized. Although I can fully understand the excitement of the children, the first step of good chicken keeping is to maintain a quiet and calm manner, and this needs to be explained from day one. Respecting any animal is a must.

TOP: A lovely alert hybrid hen.
BOTTOM LEFT: An ideal box
to transport your girls home in.
BOTTOM RIGHT: A point-of-lay hybrid
ready to go to a new home.

TRANSPORTING YOUR CHICKENS

Pet carriers are good for bringing home your chickens, but if you don't have one, a cardboard box is also excellent. It needs plenty of air holes cut into it so the chickens can breathe – these can be made simply by pushing in scissors and turning. Shredded newspaper makes good bedding and can be disposed of when you have finished with it. It is best for your chickens to travel together in one box if possible, because it is less scary when they're with their friends! It is not acceptable to tie the chickens' legs together and put them in the trunk of the car, and neither is placing them in burlap sacks. One family thought it was fine to let their children hold the chickens on their laps in the car, although boxes were provided. This, of course, would be dangerous.

SETTLING THEM IN

Once home with your girls, place them into the coop and leave them quietly for about an hour— or half an hour if it is a hot day. Be careful when opening the box to transfer them to the coop because they can sometimes jump out. I can remember one Saturday taking a telephone call from a lady who had bought her chickens from us that morning. Her White Leghorn had jumped out of the box and run off. She thought it might run back to me, but I explained that it was highly unlikely because she lived 20 miles away!

Keep other pets and children away, and after about an hour you can let the chickens out. They might be reluctant at first, but resist the urge to push them. Be patient, and they will eventually come, especially for a treat if they are being particularly stubborn! If possible, sit with them for a while so that they can get familiar with you.

Once they have been out and fed and have scratched around, calmly introduce any pets, but do it responsibly and carefully. It needs to be a gradual process and occasionally takes a while; but if done calmly and confidently, all should be well. Screaming and overreacting to a situation will just cause more stress and anxiety.

THE FIRST NIGHT

Sometimes chickens can be quite confused about going to bed on their first night. If you place them in their coop and leave them for a while to come out on their own, they will usually remember where to go. But some girls can be nervous and have no idea. The only option is to physically pick them up and put them back in the coop yourself. You should need to do this only for a couple of nights at most. Another option is to place a lamp in the coop so the light can be seen through the pop hole. It works, but again, not on all girls.

Handling

Handling chickens is an important part of poultry keeping and should be done regularly and with confidence. When you purchase your chickens, ask the seller to show you how to do it. One of the best ways to learn the art of handling correctly is to watch it being done. The key to handling your chickens successfully is to do it slowly and confidently, while talking to them softly. Any shouting or fast movements will alarm them and should be avoided. Handling them at night is always preferable because they will be calm and less likely to fly off. Talk to them as you approach, and handle them gently. You are aiming to slide your hand in under their breast so you end up cradling them. Place your thumb over one wing, and tuck the other wing into your body. The more practice you have of this, the better you will become. If it is done calmly, your birds will soon realize that you mean no harm and react accordingly.

Chickens are sensitive to their immediate surroundings. They can become stressed if kept in a coop and run that are of inadequate size, if they are handled roughly, or if they are living near young or unruly dogs. Do you have young children who might tease them or are loud? Lack of food and water will cause them stress, as will hot weather with no shade or cold weather with no shelter. Are predators pestering them at night scratching at their coop? This, too, will make them anxious.

I once had a phone call from a lady who was perturbed because her hens had stopped laying for no discernable reason, and she had only had them for two months. It seems that her Labrador had been chasing them and had actually caught one. I explained that, although none were hurt, the stress of the incident would certainly have caused the lack of eggs. Chickens can become used to dogs barking and children playing, even the noise of helicopters overhead, but anything that makes them uneasy can cause them to become stressed, and stress can affect their health. They will remember stressful incidents for a while, but it is possible to rekindle the lost trust with time and patience.

RIGHT: How to hold a chicken correctly, making it feel safe and secure.

CHILDREN AND CHICKENS

Having grown up with chickens, my children are all rather blasé about the whole thing. I have come to realize that children are normally far more resilient than we give them credit for, and keeping chickens has given me the opportunity to deal with subjects such as death, illness, and reproduction. We have had tears and laughter.

My youngest learned a very hard lesson on gentle handling when his excitement got the better of him and he accidentally hugged a chick to death – something he will never forget or do again. But death is something we all have to deal with at some point, and encountering it with a pet allows children to understand that it is perfectly natural.

We have had all sorts of pets in our house, and I can honestly say that chickens are the best. They let you cuddle them; they follow you; and they even join in when you are in the garden, in their own way. And they produce eggs for breakfast.

The children have also benefitted at school because a lot of schools are now showing children about incubation. My youngest daughter's confidence was given a huge boost when she became the chicken guru in her class. I have had several visits from local schools, and the joy and enthusiasm shown by the children gives me a real buzz. A little boy who was buying some hens for himself asked me why farmers think it's OK to keep chickens in cages. Both his mother and I were amazed that a small child realized that this is wrong. A couple of boys who bought chickens from me are making a reasonable return on their investment by selling the eggs. They even phoned me to ask if they could buy trays of eggs from me because they couldn't keep up with the demand and were getting a better price than I was selling my eggs for. I definitely see them as entrepreneurs of the future!

Children are perfectly capable of looking after chickens, but they need a responsible adult overseeing them and— I have found— occasional nagging to do the chores.

OPPOSITE AND ABOVE: Children love chickens and benefit from the responsibility of owning a productive pet.

There are more chickens on earth than there are people.

INTRODUCING ADDITIONAL CHICKENS TO YOUR FLOCK

It is not a good idea to add adult chickens to an established flock for bio-security reasons: it is the easiest way to introduce parasites and disease to your flock. This is not a recommended practice. Unless new pullets are from the same place from which you obtained your original chickens, you should keep them separate for up to a month to observe them and make sure they are disease free. When you are sure that they are healthy, it's time to introduce them to the existing flock. If you have a lot of space or your girls are free ranging, I would choose to do this at night when the older girls are settled. Sprinkling mite powder or garlic on them so they all smell the same will help. In the morning when you let them out, put extra food and water dishes in the run (temporarily) to dilute any territory issues; hang up some distractions (page 34); add a few logs; and change the run as much as possible so that the older chickens are slightly unsure as well. Make sure you're around for the day to keep an eye on them. If you have a rooster in your flock, the hens will normally settle quickly. A flock consisting of all girls can take a good week to settle. Introducing new chickens to a small run is slightly more stressful, both for you and them. Distractions and treats help to occupy the girls but will not eliminate the arguments as they try to establish the new pecking order. (See page 94.) If possible, make a second small temporary run near the main run so that the girls can see each other and sleep together for a while before the final introduction. I find moving the new chickens into the original run and the old ones into the temporary run for a day or so will also help. It is always best to introduce two chickens at the same time for obvious reasons.

RIGHT: My Jack Russell enjoying an afternoon snack with the girls.

INTRODUCING CHICKENS TO OTHER PETS

When introducing your dog, have it on a lead and walk around the enclosure. If it barks and lunges, reprimand it firmly and walk away from the coop. It takes a while for dogs to settle with something new, but normally one peck from a chicken is enough. I have a Jack Russell and an English Bull Terrier, both of which wouldn't dream of touching any of my girls. I am, however, a great believer of firm handling with my dogs. My Jack Russell has even been known to share her dinner with Gertie, one of my Silkies. Remember, it is never advisable to leave your dogs totally unsupervised.

Cats are normally fine with chickens – if you log on to YouTube, you will see that it is the chicken that always appears to be in charge. There are, however, instances when a local tom cat might cause problems. It is not a common problem, but one to bear in mind.

Keep in mind that if your chickens are too comfortable around your dogs and cats, they may not see other animals as a threat and may become easy prey to outside dogs or other predators.

Can you keep rabbits and guinea pigs with chickens? Yes, but you need sufficient space and areas where the guinea pigs and rabbits can be by themselves, and the chickens cannot get to them. A peck from a chicken can injure a small animal more than you might think.

RAISING YOUR OWN CHICKS

By far the best way to hatch and rear chicks is nature's way – a broody hen. Silkies, Cochins, Sussex, and certain crossbreeds are fantastic mothers and are a joy to watch. The other option is to use an incubator. There are some very good ones on the market, so do your research and buy the best one you can afford. Bear in mind that eggs need turning at least three times a day at regular intervals. An automatic incubator will turn the eggs for you. Read the instructions for your new incubator thoroughly, and follow them. You will need to place it in a room where the temperature is constant, away from direct sunlight, which will cause the temperature to rise. Disinfect your incubator before use, and run it for at least 24 hours, checking the temperature and humidity levels before use. The humidity level needs to be around 55%. Once the correct levels have been reached, you can place your eggs inside. Eggs should be as fresh as possible and disinfected with a product that is suitable for both eggs and incubator.

Candling

The temperature should be 99.5°F for the first 17 days. The humidity needs to be around 55% up until day 17. Those levels are from my own experience using my incubators. Always read the manufacturer's guidelines, and follow them because the levels will vary according to the type of incubator.

When the eggs have been in the incubator for about six days, you need to *candle* them. This involves holding the egg against a bright light so you can view the contents. You can make your own by placing a lamp inside a cardboard box that has a hole cut in it. It's best to do this in a darkened room. It is important to check the eggs' fertility at this stage, as infertile eggs can explode and contaminate the incubator.

Candling also allows you to monitor the humidity levels by checking the air cell in the egg. If the air cell is too small, it means that the humidity is too high. If it is too large, the humidity is too low, and you will need to adjust the level accordingly by adding or taking water away. Infertile eggs will appear clear and, again, should be removed because they can become rotten and explode. Those that are fertile will have a small, dark blob with veins coming out, rather like a thin petal on a flower. Eggs that have a dark circle inside can also be discarded. I candle again at 14 days to check that everything is all right, and then I leave the eggs alone.

ABOVE: A mixture of purebred chicks chilling out on my daughter's lap.

Hatching

At 18 days, stop turning the eggs so that the chicks can get into the correct position to hatch. The first sign of hatching is called *pipping* – this is where the chick breaks through the membrane and makes a small hole in the shell. You will be able to hear the chicks chirping to each other, and if you speak to them, they will answer you!

It can take a chick about 24 hours to hatch from its first pipping to coming completely out of the shell, though some seem to do it in a matter of hours.

It is not advisable to help out the chicks – there is usually a reason for them having difficulty. It could be that there are problems with the temperature or humidity levels or simply that it was not meant to be. Late hatches (when the chick takes longer than 21 days) are usually because the temperature is too low. It may not grow well, have thin legs with crooked toes, or might not be able to learn to eat or drink. If the temperature is too high, the chicks will hatch early (before 21 days), and they can suffer from splayed legs. (See page 132.) If this happens you will need to adjust the temperature and humidity levels when you hatch again. Keep records of any changes you make and what the results are. You will eventually reach an optimal formula to get your best hatch. It will take time. I have had my incubators for years and know them as well as my husband.

Eggs can withstand drops in temperature better than increases, so if there is a power outage don't panic. If the power is going to be off for a short while, cover the incubators with towels or an old blanket/sleeping bag to prevent as much heat loss as possible. Contact the utility company to check how long the power is going to be off. If it is for a long time, place the eggs in a box; wrap it in a towel; and put it somewhere warm. Your hatch rate might not be very good, but it's worth a try, especially if the eggs are ready to hatch.

I have had a chick hatch in my bra before. When checking on one of my broody hens one morning, she had given up and left her nest. Two chicks were half out of the shells but stone cold and apparently lifeless, another one had a faint chirping coming from it, so I put them all in my bra and continued to go about my morning jobs. By about 10 o'clock the chirps were becoming louder and more determined. By 2 PM I had two lovely fluffy girls scratching around, closely followed by number three a couple of hours later. Needless to say, they didn't stay there for long!

It is truly amazing to watch a chick hatch – even my teenage son cannot resist a look and is often found in the incubator room, saying he's looking for a bicycle pump.

Raising

Once your chicks have hatched and dried in the incubator, they should be moved into their new home. I find raising them in large plastic boxes works well for me because they are both easy to clean and draftproof. I line the bottom with a layer of newspaper covered with textured paper towels or cheese cloth for the first week to prevent the chicks' developing splayed legs due to the floor being too slippery. (See page 132.)

It is important to keep the chicks warm. This is done by suspending a heat lamp above the box. (Make sure that the heat lamp is secured at least 24 inches away from anything flammable.) You will know when your chicks are at the right temperature by their behavior. If they are all huddled together under the heat lamp, they are too cold; if they are all round the edge of the box, trying to get away from the heat, they are too hot. Avoid both scenarios.

Chicks kept at the right temperature will be happy walking around and sleeping where they drop. Most heat lamps come with a chain from which to hang the lamp, which makes adjusting the heat easy. Simply raise the lamp if the chicks appear to be too hot or lower it if they seem too cold. You are aiming to harden them by about four to five weeks, but this will depend a bit on the weather and the time of year. Keep chicks at 92°F–95°F for the first week. Then decline the temperature by 5°F per week until they reach room or environmental temperature.

Ideally hatching is best done in the spring, as Mother Nature intended, because of all of the natural benefits: good weather, fresh grass, an abundance of bugs, and longer days to eat and grow.

On the fourth or fifth week, turn off the lamp during the day, but turn it back on at night for a week. Then stop the heat lamp altogether. If you are raising your chicks in colder months, you will have to use your own judgment on lengths of time, but remember that the tougher they are from an early age, the hardier the adult bird.

Chicks need to be fed on medicated starter crumble. It is very small and contains all the nutrients they need. Check the label, and make sure it contains anti-coccidiosis. Coccidiosis is a disease that can be fatal in chicks. (See page 128.) I place the crumble in chick feeders, but for the first couple of days I also sprinkle a little around the chicks and try to encourage them to eat, rather like a mother hen would do. They don't take long to get the hang of eating and drinking.

When they are six days old, stop using paper towels and add a small amount of pine shavings instead. Clean out the boxes regularly because dirty, damp litter can cause multiple problems.

PROS AND CONS OF RAISING CHICKS

Pros
- Great fun and rewarding
- Educational for children
- Produces great chickens

Cons
- You get cockerels
- Time consuming
- Requires additional housing
- Deaths due to disease and/ or power outages

Do not count your
chickens before
they are hatched
— Aesop

You need to make sure that water is available at all times. Special chick waterers are available that work well. Otherwise you can use small plant saucers, but make sure you add clean pebbles to prevent the chicks from drowning. Waterers should be placed on raised wire. This can easily be done – screw four pieces of batten together to form a small square, and tack wire tightly over the top. This stops the litter from clogging them up as the chicks scratch.

Change the water regularly – about three times a day – because it can become warm under the heat lamps. After about a week, start adding very small amounts of flint grit to their food to help the digestion process. Don't add oyster shell because the extra calcium in the diet at this age will cause bone-development problems and can damage their kidneys.

At six weeks the chicks should be out in their own coop. If possible, move the run regularly to avoid any problems, and protect the chicks from the elements as you would adult girls.

They should now be fed with grower's crumbles until they are 18 weeks old. Do this by gradually mixing half chick crumbles and half grower's crumbles for a week. Add a peeled clove of garlic to the water in the container. Worming is a must when you put the chicks into their outside coop. Verm-X is my preferred wormer, and for chicks I use the liquid form, which can be added to the drinking water or soaked into bread. Make sure the chicks are in a covered run because they can easily be taken by aerial predators such as hawks, falcons, and crows.

Daily
care and
behavior

Routine

TOP LEFT: A beautiful Cochin hen. TOP RIGHT: Topping up feeders with a scoop makes life much easier. BOTTOM LEFT: Collecting eggs daily reduces the chance of accidental breakage. BOTTOM RIGHT: Different colored eggs make an attractive display in any kitchen.

So you've set up the coop, and your chickens have been happily introduced to their new home. Once your girls are settled, you will find that they will thrive on routine; it makes them feel safe and confident, so start the way you mean to go on. Your daily routine will continue throughout the year. The only change will be the times at which you do things, which are dependent on the season. There is no need to set your alarm and be up at the crack of dawn. If anything, I advise you to wait until the world is awake in the hope that any predators have gone to bed, but bear in mind that they're not teenagers, so they won't appreciate being left in until midday. The time they go to bed also changes according to the seasons, so I go out first before dark to watch and wait. It won't always be possible to stick rigidly to your routine, and the occasional deviation is fine – if you are planning to go out for the evening, for example, put them to bed before you go. They won't be that eager, but much better this than being eaten by a predator.

Once you've unlocked your chickens, they will need fresh water. They drink a lot, so in hot weather you may need to replenish their supply in the afternoon as well as in the morning. I believe in feeding my girls on a regular basis; I top up their feeders every day so they have food available all the time. The girls eat what they need and in my experience are not overly greedy. Their food intake varies according to weather conditions, with their requiring more food in the winter to stay warm. Layer's crumbles have everything in them to keep the girls healthy and produce delicious eggs. With this done, just look around the run perimeters to check that no predators have been around.

After your chickens have had their breakfast and a stretch, they will go off to lay their eggs, so give them an hour or so and then collect them. You should avoid letting the eggs build up over a few days because if you do, they can break and, once broken, the chickens won't be able to resist eating them. Once started, this habit can be very difficult to stop.

In the afternoon/early evening, your chickens will appreciate a treat such as a handful of mixed corn. This is a great time to tame them. Just call them over or shake the bucket before scattering, and they will associate the noise with the treat and come running. If your chickens are out and you need to get them back in, throwing a small handful of corn onto the floor of the run will tempt them back in, and it makes them scratch and forage, a good, natural behavior. But be sparing with the "treats."

Remember, that to chickens corn is like chocolate, and fat chickens do not lay many eggs! I recently had a customer come to the farm complaining that one of his girls wasn't laying. When I took the box from him to have a look at her, I thought he had several hens in there, but instead there was just one very happy but enormous girl. After a strict diet she started laying again.

If you have any scraps of vegetables, fruit, pasta, rice, and the like, mid-afternoon is the time to feed them to your chickens. If possible, hang them so the girls have to reach for them – a bit like a workout. This is a great time to watch their antics, establish who the boss is, and check that they are okay. Just before dusk, lock up your girls. In the early days of having them, you may find that they are slightly confused and need some persuading. Calmly and slowly ushering them with open arms usually works.

Once they're in for the night, it's always a good idea to clear away any uneaten scraps and treats so as not to attract rodents. Double-check the lock, and the job's done.

This is much easier to do without a glass of wine, as my friend happily does every night to escape the chaos of the house!

If you are around in the garden during the day, the girls will always appreciate a stroll around the garden with you. But be warned that they will eat your plants and, once settled, will think nothing of going into your house for a look around. You should never leave them in the garden out of their run without your being around, as it only takes a minute for a predator to pay a visit, as I know from personal experience.

TIMETABLE

Early morning: Unlock your chickens; feed them; and give them fresh water.

Mid-morning: Collect eggs.

Afternoon/early evening: Offer your chickens a treat.

Dusk: Lock up your girls; clear away uneaten scraps; and check the coop perimeter.

RIGHT: A black sex-link enjoying a supervised afternoon free range.

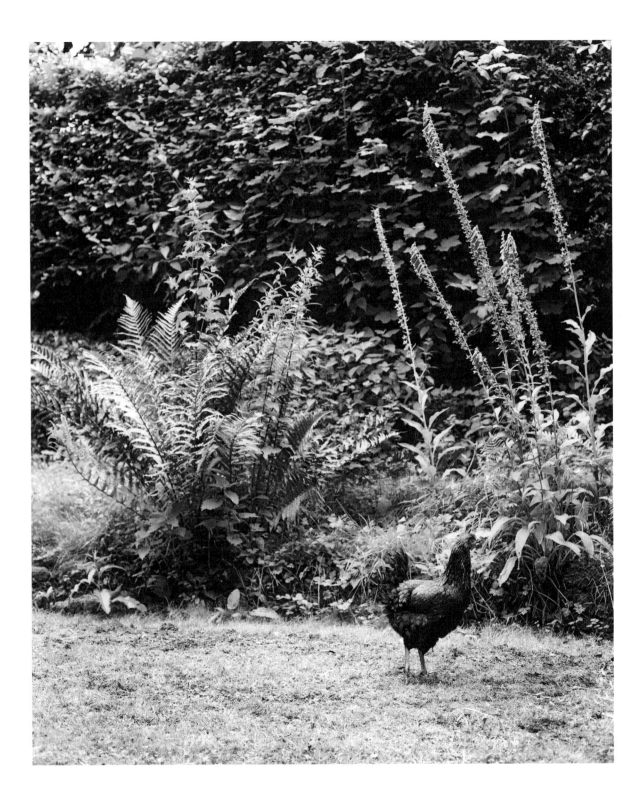

Going on vacation

The first time you leave your girls to go on vacation is worrying, but it can be simple with the correct planning. If you are going away just for the weekend, they should be fine if left with ample food and water. This is, of course, presuming the house and run are predator-proof. Make thorough checks of the coop and perimeter before you leave. It is a good idea to hang some vegetables in the run for their entertainment.

If you plan to leave them for a week or more, you will need to give it slightly more thought. Neighbors are usually willing to check daily and replenish food and water in return for the delicious eggs. But if neighbors or friends can't help out, try putting an advertisement in the local newspaper. Pet shops may know of people who will come to your house or provide lodging while you are away. Be cautious of the latter because, if other poultry are at the temporary home, diseases can be caught.

The day before you leave, give the coop a good cleaning; then you need not worry until you come back. Check that you have left enough food, grit, and treats to last and that you have explained the routine to the person caring for them. The chickens may become bored, as they will not be out roaming, so hanging vegetables and toys is a must to keep them amused.

It is also a good idea to leave a simple checklist of dos and don'ts, plus the number of the local vet in case of problems.

CHECKLIST FOR "CHICKEN SITTERS"

It sounds obvious, but remember to leave a contact number in case of emergency.
Also:
- Make sure they know where the hens' food is kept.
- Make sure they understand your chickens' routine – when to lock up and let them out.
- And remind them NOT TO LET THE CHICKENS OUT OF THE RUN UNSUPERVISED.

RIGHT: An inquisitive black sex-link.

Care and maintenance

WEEKLY MAINTENANCE

Once a week you need to rake out large waste. Air the coop for an hour or two. Make sure the pop hole is closed, as the girls will not miss an opportunity to escape! On one particularly beautiful day I left the door and nest boxes open in one of my large laying houses that had 50 girls in, and didn't close the pop hole. So I had 50 girls scattered everywhere. Luckily, when I approached the chickens with a bucket of food, they came running and followed me as if I were the Pied Piper.

When the coop has had a good airing, remember to open the pop hole. Also disinfect your waterer – in hot weather it will become slimy and green. If you have a fixed run, rake over the ground and if possible add a log (page 38) – something to make it slightly different for the chickens. If it's a movable run, place it on fresh ground – this is much easier to do when the girls are loaded into their house. Check your perimeters for any signs of wear and tear or predators. Top up the feed, and your job is nearly finished. It is advisable to regularly check where you store your bedding and chicken feed; this is often overlooked, until, one day, you are greeted with a gnawed storage bin and a pile of droppings. Move your containers, and check for signs of droppings and chew marks; lift up the bedding, and have a good look for any signs of rodents. If you find any, you need to put down some bait, set a trap, or call an exterminator. Put all of your tools away; sit down with a cup of coffee, and watch your girls' excitement over their clean home. We live in a busy world, but I cannot emphasize enough the joy your girls will give you if you spend time with them. Try it; you won't be disappointed – it's much better than daytime TV – and while watching, check that they all appear in good health.

REGULAR TASKS

WEEKLY
Rake large waste; clean waterers; check for signs of rodents/predators.

MONTHLY
Weather permitting, clean and disinfect; treat girls and house for mites; disinfect waterers; air the house thoroughly; worm the girls if necessary using Verm-X.

YEARLY
Treat the house with wood preserver; general maintenance of the run and house, hinges, locks, etc.

TOP LEFT: Some young Buff Orpington pullets checking out blackberries hung up for entertainment. BOTTOM LEFT: Verm-X natural wormer is easy and safe to give. FAR RIGHT: Home-grown lavender. My daughter dries it out and makes lavender bags, which she pins inside the coops to make them smell nice and help the chickens relax.

MONTHLY MAINTENANCE

The first day of every month is a very busy one on the farm. It's deep-clean day, health-check day, and worming day. This may sound daunting, but it is great fun, and after years of doing the same routine, I still get a buzz and sense of achievement when all the jobs are done – and I certainly sleep well afterward.

If you have chosen a wooden house with a permanent floor, it's a good idea to purchase some inexpensive sheet flooring. Cut two pieces to size so they fit in the bottom of the coop. When cleaning, you can roll the sides up and empty the mess straight into the compost or trash can. The second piece can be placed into the coop while you clean and dry the dirty piece. Use a paint scraper to clean off the chicken droppings.

You need to move your house if it is movable, remembering to keep your chickens locked up in the coop. Disinfect your waterer and feeder; refill them; and put them back into the run. If you use Verm-X wormer, as I do, put the dose into the feeder. Once this is done, catch your girls one by one and give them a good check, looking for signs of mites and injury. Are their feathers looking good? Is their comb nice and red? Are their legs nice and smooth? How does their weight feel?

You will, after doing this regularly, begin to know what is right for your birds. Before putting them into the run, check to see whether there are any problems.

The girls will now be happily having breakfast, so you need to empty the coop of bedding. If the weather is dry and sunny, spray the house with mite treatment, and allow it to dry by airing. When it is dry, scatter Diatom Powder around (page 124), and place some fresh bedding inside. Open the pop hole, and check all the hinges and locks – if they are starting to rust, smear them with grease. Check that the perimeters of the run are fixed, and look for signs of rodents around the coop, particularly if it is on the ground. Deal with any problems as you find them. Do not be tempted to leave it for another day, as you may lose your girls.

If you have a fixed run, you need to rake it over thoroughly, removing any heavily soiled areas, and spray with a disinfectant. If it's very wet, you might need to add wood bark to make the environment nicer for the girls. While they like paddling in mud, they don't wipe their feet and will track mud into the coop, which will add to your cleaning tasks. Wood bark is not expensive and works very well – the girls can still scratch and forage – and don't forget to add some enriching toys (page 38). If you have a dust bath, top it up and add mite powder to it. Finally, disinfect all of the tools you have used, and put them away, checking your storage area for rodent activity.

CAN I BATHE MY CHICKENS?

Yes, but usually chickens keep themselves clean and do not require any help. When people show their birds, they usually bathe them. If you are going to wash a chicken, have two bowls of warm water ready. Place the bird in one; wet it thoroughly; and use a small amount of baby shampoo to wash it. You need to do this calmly, talking softly to your bird. Try to hold the bird with one hand and wash it with the other – this takes practice, and you will get wet if you do not keep the wings tucked in. Rinse well, and gently pat the bird dry using a towel. You can use a hair dryer on a low setting, following the direction of the feathers. Hard-feathered breeds are best left to dry naturally. Remember that bathing is usually done only when showing the birds. If you bathe those you keep as pets for eggs, the stress can stop them from laying.

RIGHT: Blow-drying a Polish hen after her bath.

LEFT: Suspending a feeder in the run
helps to prevent the girls from spilling
food and attracting vermin.

PEST CONTROL

It is said that we are never far from a rat. Rats and mice can be a problem when keeping chickens, but only if you are messy with their food and do not clear away uneaten treats. It is this that attracts them, not the chickens. Debris left around the coop and log piles can provide perfect nesting sites, so keep these areas clear, and put stored feed in metal containers to avoid any trouble. You are legally required to keep rodents under control, and because they breed so quickly, this can be a constant battle. Methods of control are traps, either live-catch ones, which catch them humanely, or impact, which kill; bait, which poisons them; or Harry, my exterminator!

Traps can be purchased from most hardware stores, pet shops, and home centers, or via the Internet. You need to follow the instructions carefully. If you are using live-catch traps, think about how you are going to kill the pest once you've caught it. You need to kill them humanely. (You can also drive to a remote area and release them.) Impact traps work effectively, but you need to be careful when setting them because you don't want to catch birds/cats/dogs/your child's guinea pig.

Traps need to be placed where you can see that the pests have been active – they are very wary of new things, so rub your new traps in your chickens' bedding or the compost heap, or leave it outside for a few days. Do not site traps in the open because rodents tend to make their runs in sheltered areas.

There are lots of poisons on the market to use as bait, and I have tried most. They work quickly (between one and four days), but they present a risk to other creatures. Also, you cannot predict where the pest will die – it could be under the floorboards of your house. Poisons need to be used carefully. You must follow the instructions on handling and usage to the letter.

I have always disposed of the rodent carcasses by wrapping the body in a plastic bag, securing it, then placing it in a rigid container that can be put in the trash. Your local regulations for disposal may be different, so check. Always wear gloves, as rodents can pose a health risk even when dead.

For a reasonable fee, Harry has taken on my vermin control. His knowledge and equipment are a godsend, and I wish I had found him years ago. Bear in mind that by the time you have bought your traps or bait and spent time positioning them, waiting, and maybe catching a bird or two by mistake, it might be more economical to find a local exterminator.

Over the years I have used all the methods of rodent control mentioned, even paid my sons money per pest caught dead. I have had great success with all of the methods mentioned.

ABOVE: Placing concrete slabs around runs helps prevent predators from digging their way in.

PREDATORS

Predators such as foxes, coyotes, and dogs are a constant problem. Making sure the coop/run is predator-proof is my biggest job. Wiring the bottom of the run can be done easily but affects the chickens' ability to scratch, so it is not something I favor. Instead, if you have a movable run, put skirts of wire around the edges, and secure them with tent stakes. This works well if you have a fixed permanent run. Concrete slabs (left) are excellent because they stop any predators from digging underneath and give you a path around which to walk, making checking the perimeter easy and mud free!

Human hair is said to be a deterrent – hairdressers are usually happy to supply you with this. You can stuff the hair into old stockings and hang them from the run. There are also products on the market for scaring predators, which use lights and/or ultrasonic sounds.

Even if you think you have a predator-proof home, change your routine occasionally. Let the chickens out later, or put them to bed earlier. Sometimes leave a radio on, or place a solar garden light nearby, or rattle cans hung to fences – something new will keep the predators on their toes.

Electric fencing (page 27) is used by many chicken keepers, including me. This works well – but there is always a but! Maintenance is important. In order for an electric fence to work correctly, it needs to be set up properly and the manufacturer's instructions followed. The area directly under the electric fence needs to be clear of anything that could ground the electric current. Long grass should be regularly strimmed/cut and cleared away, and you need to check every day for anything that might have fallen on the wire. I check my fences daily with a current tester to make sure sufficient current is passing around the fence – when there is, it is an effective deterrent.

Most faults are simple to fix, but when there is a problem your chickens are vulnerable. I have kept chickens for many years and have had my fair share of disasters, mainly due to foxes – sometimes because of my own stupidity and other times due to the fox's cunning persistence. On one occasion I had been having my morning cup of coffee watching my girls (45 stunning Buff Orpington pullets) that were coming on tremendously well. I was so proud having hatched and reared them, and because I was with them I had switched off the electric fence. I was sitting there happily watching them frolic and play, when the phone rang. I left them for all of 20 minutes while I chatted to a customer, and was in the office (barn), not more than 40 yards away, where they were just out of sight. The customer was enquiring about my birds, and when I finished speaking and started to walk back to the girls, I realized something was wrong.

A fox had jumped the fence and killed all but two of them, which I had to dispatch because of their injuries. I strongly believe he was watching me, saw his opportunity, and took it. So never let your guard down because this is when they strike.

On another occasion I had seen some signs of digging around my Brahmas' cage. I had meant to inspect it more closely, but my children distracted me and I forgot – unfortunately the chickens paid the price that night with their lives. It would have been only a quick job because the fence just needed to be staked down. If only I had done it!

Whatever your view is of foxes, it is your responsibility to protect your girls. It is not a good idea to feed foxes in your garden if you have chickens, which some of my customers do, as it really is asking for trouble. It is a fox's natural instinct to hunt and kill, even on a full stomach.

Remember that you can fox-proof your coop and run, and put up lots of deterrents, but if you don't close the door, you've lost the battle. It might sound silly, but believe me, it happens regularly. I recall a morning when I noticed the three men who work on the farm walking briskly in my direction. This was very unusual; they don't usually move that quickly! "This one needs you," they said, and as I walked down the drive to investigate, I found a customer coming up the drive crying. She told me that she had not closed her coop properly and had lost all her chickens to the fox.

Seasonal care

Spring

In the spring, the weather is improving; the garden is coming to life; and for me, this is a magical time of year. The hard winter is behind us, and at last, hopefully, a few months of good weather lay ahead. It is a busy time of year on the farm, and early spring is spent mending fencing runs and generally cleaning up. Now is a good time to do any maintenance on the chickens' run and do any reseeding, as long as the frost appears to have finished.

The girls will be eager to get out and about. Check the coop for any mites or damage, and treat appropriately. This is when pests begin to breed, so clear away any debris that might become nesting sites. Be aware that fox cubs are being born and soon they will be out hunting. I find foxes become really desperate toward the end of spring, when the cubs are weaned from their mother but are not quite old enough to hunt for themselves.

Summer

In summer, with lovely long, hot days, life can be wonderful, and it is easy to think we can just sit back and enjoy it. Unfortunately, these days are perfect for mites to breed. Summer showers can cause warm, damp, humid conditions that in turn can be the perfect breeding ground for disease. There is little we can do about the weather, but routine jobs and tricks can make life a lot easier.

Check for mites, and if found, treat them immediately and thoroughly (page 124). Clean waterers regularly because algae can form quickly. If you wouldn't drink the water, replace it! Make sure the chickens have adequate shade – heat stroke can occur, and they can dehydrate quickly (page 130). Small water bottles frozen overnight and placed in the run can be used by the chickens to lay on and cool down! Some love it; others don't. Some love to be sprayed with a fine mist of water.

Citronella is good if sprayed around the coop to deter flies. Fly traps hung close by (but out of the reach of the chickens) work well. Make sure you worm your girls regularly. Toward the end of summer and into the early autumn is when most chickens go through the annual molt, when they naturally lose their feathers and replace them with new ones. A chicken going through its first molt may lose only a few feathers, but the second and subsequent molts can be quiet dramatic and alarming to a new chicken keeper. With pure breeds, egg laying slows or stops when the chicken is molting; with hybrids, depending on their age, laying may continue. The annual molt can take 8–14 weeks to complete. If a chicken is still laying while going through the molt, it can put a huge drain on her. It takes a lot to stay healthy and lay eggs as well as replace feathers. Feathers are made of keratin, a fibrous protein, so adding this to the diet is beneficial.

A daily fresh mix of oats, seaweed, cod liver oil, garlic, and a little water is a great help when fed in the early afternoon toward the end of summer and autumn. If you collect berries, the girls will love a few of these. For a cooling summer treat, freeze them in individual ice-cube trays, and toss one or two into the run on hot, sunny days. If you collect lots, freeze some and bring them out in the dull winter months. The chickens will love you for it – just make sure the berries are defrosted.

Autumn

Some chickens may just be starting their annual molt, while some will be coming to the end (page 114). Check all fencing and the coops for signs of wear, and mend where appropriate. You don't want to be doing these jobs in the winter, when the days are shorter.

Your girls may have stopped laying or are laying sporadically. This is perfectly normal for older girls and pure breeds, but unless there is a dramatic change in the weather, spring-hatched hybrids should continue to lay. Quite a few poultry keepers will restock with a few young chickens at this time of year to see them through the winter months.

Keeping chickens at a minimum of 14 hours of light allows them to lay year round. Always add light to the morning hours. Turn off lights at sunrise, and let the chicken go to roost naturally at sunset. As the leaves start to fall, you can collect them and place them in piles in the outside runs. This gives the girls a fresh place to scratch, and you can replenish them whenever you need to.

If you can find an alternative temporary coop, such as a playhouse, garage, or even greenhouse, and put in suitable bedding, you could treat the main coop with wood preserver, which is beneficial. Also check that there are no leaks in the roof. When the house is completely dry and well aired, replace the chickens, ready for the winter.

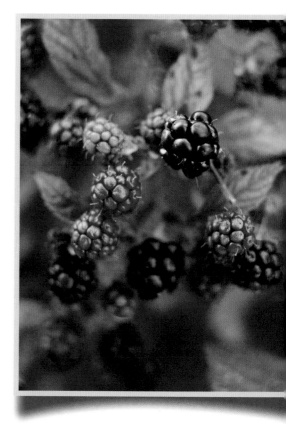

ABOVE: Blackberries can be harvested and frozen to provide treats throughout the year.

Winter

During the winter you need to continue making checks on perimeter fences because, as the days become colder, predators will become more determined and will not miss an opportunity to get in. It is useful to coat hinges and locks with grease – there is nothing worse than trying to deal with frozen hinges in the snow. You need to be particularly vigilant about rodents who are looking for spilled food and a place to live (page 87).

A lot of people leave their chickens in one place over the winter and add shelter and windbreakers to make them happier. If you decide to do this, treat the rest of your ground with a covering of lime, which will help reduce acidity in the soil. This is said to also help with internal parasites such as worms.

If you put up shelter over the run, try to make it so that you can roll it back or remove it on nice days. If there is any snow, put tarpaulins over the runs. This enables you to get the snow off in the morning and leaves you with a snow-free run and roof; it has been known for roofs on runs to collapse when snow is not removed. In extreme weather conditions when the temperature plummets, coat the chickens' wattles and combs with petroleum jelly to prevent frostbite (page 130). Check water regularly when the weather is freezing. I have found it useful to replace my hanging water fonts with shallow dishes, which are easier to empty of ice and to fill. If you make a warm meal for the girls, it will be greeted with great excitement, and it makes you feel better about them being outside. Each day, make a freshly mixed meal of boiled potato skins, bran, oats, and cod liver oil.

If the weather is freezing for prolonged periods, deep-litter the chickens. Instead of cleaning out the old bedding, put a fresh layer on top, and continue to do this until the weather breaks. Leaving the dirty bedding under the fresh will produce heat, which will rise and keep the girls warm. When the weather breaks, a thorough cleaning will be necessary. This is a method used by a lot of farmers and backyard homesteaders to keep their stock warmer.

AUTUMN
- Check for mites
- Set up artificial lights to lengthen the day (to increase the egg yield)
- Give a maintenance check to runs and coops
- Collect fallen leaves for the runs
- Treat the coop with wood preserver

WINTER
- Provide protection from the elements
- If weather is extreme, cover runs with tarpaulin and remove snow daily
- In freezing conditions, replenish water frequently
- Make constant checks for predators because they will be desperate for food
- Give brewer's yeast for a few days to combat lack of sunlight

RIGHT: Hanging greens provides entertainment and a workout for the girls.

Chicken behavior

Once you have shared your life with chickens, it is difficult to see them as anything other than members of your family. Their behavior is not dissimilar to our own – except for scratching for bugs!

Every flock of hens will have a top girl who calls all the shots. She will eat first, assume the right to have any bugs found, and have the favored perch position at night. She will also look out for her peers. As a flock, when needed, they will work together. It can be upsetting to watch the bottom girl do everything last and gaze wantonly at the worm that was not to be, but once the girls have established their place within the flock, they will settle well. A flock with all top girls would be a stressful, unhappy environment to endure. A balance will be struck, as in everyday life.

Scratching, dustbathing, preening, and sunbathing are all normal undertakings for chickens, and this is how they like to fill their days. They also argue and boss each other around, and they like to explore, given the chance. Some people say chickens are stupid. They are not. They will remember where they can escape, for example, and the location of the vegetable patch, and when to cluck and look cute for treats. Chickens are also astute at spotting signs of danger and will make alarm calls. Airplanes, however, freak them out and send them running for cover.

Laying their eggs is always an exciting part of the girls' day and evokes gregarious clucks of achievement, which always manages to make me smile. Once you start watching your hens, the time flies; their antics are hilarious.

Chickens use their eyes independently, and in daylight they have very good eyesight and can see different colors well. In stark contrast, they are almost blind at night, so that is the time to catch and handle your birds. It is much easier for you and the bird. They have a special ability to feel vibrations from the ground, which helps them when foraging to sense predators or danger. If you walk up to your coop quietly at night, you will immediately hear the warning calls of your girls as they feel you coming.

CHICKEN SAYINGS

Several common sayings we use daily come from our observations of chickens, including:

- To clip someone's wings
- Pecking order
- Cockiness
- To ruffle someone's feathers
- Nest egg
- Beady eyes
- To chicken out
- To take someone under your wing
- To get in a flap

RIGHT: Hens enjoying a dust bath, which helps to keep their feathers in tip-top condition.

Studying cows, pigs, and chickens can help an actor develop his character. James Dean

LEFT: A Bearded Buff Laced Polish rooster leaping onto a stable door.

Chickens have a good sense of hearing. You will notice the different calls they make, from alarm calls to clucks of pleasure. Mother hen and her chicks are a joy to watch, and she's very vocal as she teaches her youngsters what to eat and where to scratch.

If you have a rooster in your flock, you will notice his different calls, from "cock-a-doodle-doo" (i.e., look at me) to a low mumble when he finds a tasty morsel to eat.

Chickens develop their own routines. When you let them out first thing in the morning, they are full of life, ready for a drink and something to eat. They then settle in for a day of meandering around looking for a tasty morsel to eat, dustbathing, and preening their feathers. The occasional argument may develop if one of them finds a bug and doesn't eat it quickly enough. Napping is common if the girls are comfortable in their group. When you give them their treats in the afternoon, activity starts again. As they fill their crops for the night ahead, you might notice the lower-ranked girls going to bed first in a bid to get the best perch, only to lose their place when the higher-ranked girls go inside and make them move. They will only go to sleep when it is absolutely dark and silent and will wake at the slightest noise or vibration.

A chicken can peck another for no apparent reason other than to show that it is stronger. Problems can occur when insufficient numbers of chickens are kept together. A lady calls me constantly about her two girls because only one of them gets pecked. I have explained about the pecking order and how difficult it is to establish this with only two chickens. It really is best to keep a minimum of three hens together. One more doesn't make much difference to your chores or feed bill, but it does make a difference in their behavior.

Some breeds of chickens can fly much better than others, but when we say fly it is more of a gliding jump. The longest recorded flight of a chicken lasted for 13 seconds. They are not capable of sustained flight.

Broody hens

A broody hen is a chicken that wants to be a mother. Certain breeds are more likely to go broody than others— Silkies, for example. Hybrids are less likely to become broody because their main aim is to lay lots of eggs, but it is not unheard of.

I receive phone calls about broody hens that always make me smile. When I hear some people's descriptions of their broody hens' behavior it resembles that of a rabid dog more than a protective mother. Yes, they are moody and determined, but this is behavior to be admired not feared.

A broody hen will sit in her nest box and not move. Her breast will be hot and she may have plucked out some feathers to make her nest. If you approach, she will fluff up her feathers in a bid to make herself look bigger; she will almost growl at you as a warning and will peck her hardest. Just remember a peck is normally nothing more than a pinch.

If the eggs are fertile, let her remain on the nest and hatch her eggs. Eggs take 21 days to hatch (page 70). But if you haven't got a rooster with your girls, any eggs will not be fertile and won't hatch.

You can often buy fertile eggs from breeders or on the Internet. If using the Internet, remember an egg that goes through the mail might not hatch. Also, when hatching yourself, you will get cockerels — in my experience, lots of them.

If your broody hen is sitting on infertile eggs, you need to remove them and try to break the habit. Broody hens will need to be removed from the nest twice daily. Just pick her up, and put her by the food and water. She will usually defecate and trot back into her nest box. Do this in the morning and again in the afternoon when you spread corn.

If you want to break the hen's broodiness, you need to cool her down. This can be done by placing her for a while in a broody box – this normally has a wire floor so that the air can circulate and make her cool. Another method on a dry, warm day is to place her bottom in a bowl of cold water and leave her in the run, blocking off the nest box. Placing small, frozen water bottles in the nest box sometimes works. If a chicken is very determined, it can take quite a while for her to stop, so persevere. A broody hen that is left to hatch her eggs will be a sitting target for mites and will need regular de-miting with powder.

RIGHT: A broody Cochin Frizzle hen looking rather unhappy after having been removed from her nest for lunch.

Eggs

THE ANATOMY OF AN EGG

An egg is made up of three parts – the yolk, the albumen (the white of the egg), and the shell. A female chick starts life with two ovaries, but only the left one matures, while the other one withers away, or atrophies. The ovary has a clump of undeveloped ova, or yolks, which are the yellow part of the egg. When one is released, the process of making an egg begins.

The ovum travels from the ovary down the tube (oviduct) to the funnel, or infundibulum, which catches the yolk and is where fertilization of the egg takes place if a male is present in the flock. From there, the ovum travels to the magnum, where the albumen is added. The partially formed egg is then passed farther down by squeezing movements to the isthmus, where the membrane (which you notice when peeling a boiled egg) is added.

It then passes to the uterus, where the shell is formed; this can take up to 20 hours. When the egg is laid, the *bloom* (the moist coating that can just be seen as the egg is laid, and which helps to keep out bacteria) dries out. It takes around 23–32 hours for an egg to be made. In chickens that are just reaching maturity, it is not unusual for two ova to travel down the magnum at the same time, and this will give you a double yolker. It is not unheard of to have triple yolkers, which causes great excitement with my children and the dilemma of who's going to eat it! The record of nine yolks in one egg has been recorded. These incidents decline and settle as the chickens mature. Pullets can also pass soft eggs (eggs without a shell). If this happens, it is again usually because their bodies are young and the egg passes through too quickly. Only if this happens frequently is there a problem, in which case consult a vet.

If you are lucky enough to watch one of them lay an egg, it is fascinating. I have a wonderful memory of my daughter's face when she had watched her chicken lay its egg. She came to me with such a sparkle in her eyes, clutching the warm egg. Chicken keeping is a simple hobby, but it has enriched my family's lives.

Started pullets usually start laying at about 19–21 weeks, depending on the time of year. In the warmer months they can start sooner; toward the end of the year it will usually be later. Indications that your chicken is close to lay are a lovely red comb in some breeds, such as the Leghorns, and in Rhode Island Reds their legs will be yellow. Another indicator is the gap between its pelvic bones. A hen that is laying will have a gap the width of about two to three fingers.

ABOVE: The best job of the day – collecting the fresh eggs.

Before a female chicken lays her first egg, she is called a pullet; after that, she is a hen.

Egg color is often related to the color of chicken's ears – red ears generally produce brown eggs and white ears, white eggs.

It's an exciting time when you get your first chickens and are waiting for them to lay. I can still remember when I was a small child waking up first to make sure I could collect the eggs. The disappointment of discovering that there were no eggs was immense! But then there was the reignited excitement the next day when I was going to check again. It is a magical time not only for the chickens but for the adults and children sharing the experience. When your chickens start laying, their eggs can be quite small. They can also be empty, with no contents in the shell. Don't worry because this will usually sort itself out naturally, and the eggs will get bigger as the hens mature.

I got an email from a family who had purchased their chickens from me. One of the hens had laid an egg the next day, and the mother said that it was like Christmas morning in the kitchen – everyone was so excited as they boiled the precious egg and cut it into four pieces so they could all have a taste. "It was such a wonderful experience that has brought us so much joy; I wish I had done it years ago," she wrote.

You need to remember that even if you buy a chicken that is already laying, sometimes the journey home and stress of living in a new coop may interrupt her laying for a short while. Just be patient, and it will happen.

WHAT'S IN AN EGG

Eggs are mostly water – around 75% – and are composed of three main parts:

- **Shell**
- **Egg white**
- **Egg yolk**

The shell accounts for around 11% of the total weight and has tiny pores that not only allow the developing chick to obtain oxygen but also allow water and carbon dioxide to escape. The shell is generally strong, but older hens tend to produce weaker shells. The color varies according to the breed of the bird.

The color of the egg yolk is determined by the diet of the hen and is due to the presence of carotenes and any colorings added to its feed. The nutritional value of the egg is not affected by the color of the yolk.

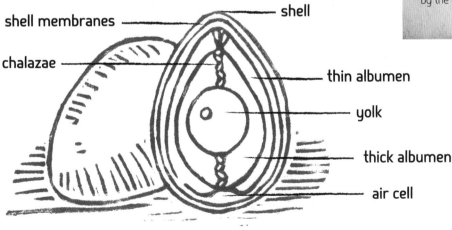

shell membranes

chalazae

shell

thin albumen

yolk

thick albumen

air cell

HOW LONG DO CHICKENS LAY EGGS?

How long a chicken will lay eggs depends on the breed. Purebred hens tend to lay seasonally, meaning that most hens come into lay in the spring, when the weather begins to get better and the days slightly longer. They continue to lay until the end of autumn, when they molt, and usually have a rest throughout the winter months. As pure breeds have natural breaks in laying, they can lay for years quite happily. My chicken Henrietta laid until she was 8½ years old, although admittedly in later years not as well as she did in her youth.

Hybrids will lay consistently for the first 12 months. Commercially they are called *spent* hens by the age of 18 months, when they are usually dispatched or re-homed. Then a new group of hens is brought in. In a domestic flock, they will begin to lay again after a break and will continue to do so for quite a few years. Most people find that killing their hens when the eggs drop off is acceptable, while others choose to keep them even though their laying is sporadic. The choice is yours. You can always introduce new hens at a later date to give you more eggs. (See page 66.)

HOW FRESH ARE YOUR EGGS?

Most "fresh" eggs bought in a supermarket are four to ten days old. To check how fresh an egg is, place it in a bowl of cold water. If it lays almost flat on the bottom, it is very fresh. If it tilts slightly fat-end up, it is older. The higher it tilts, the older the egg. If it floats on top of the water, it is very old and shouldn't be used. Be careful not to break a floater; if you do it, is guaranteed to smell horrible.

STORING YOUR EGGS

Eggs in my house are never around for long, and we keep them in a ceramic egg tray on the work surface in the kitchen. I am told that ideally they should be cleaned and stored in the fridge in an egg carton.

THE NUTRITIONAL CONTENT OF EGG YOLK

- 16.5% protein
- 33% fat
- 50% water
- Vitamins A, D, E, and K
- Mineral elements, including iron
- Lecithin (an emulsifier)

OPPOSITE: Examples of the different size eggs a chicken can lay. The bottom right egg is a pullet egg. (Do not despair; they get bigger!)

It takes about 23 to 32 hours for a chicken to lay an egg, so expect about one egg a day.

Do you need a rooster?

One of the questions I'm most frequently asked is, Do I need a rooster to make my girls lay eggs? The answer is no, your chickens will lay eggs whether you have a rooster or not. You only need a rooster if you wish to breed from your hens.

If you can have a rooster, however, it makes a nice addition to your flock. Males tend to have a calming influence on the girls and quickly break up most squabbles. They are fascinating to watch. I have had some terrific roosters. Brigadier, a huge gold Brahma, used to look after his hens like a trusted patriarch, calling them when he found a worm. His presence within the flock had a calming effect, and arguments were nonexistent. He was always last to bed, almost counting his girls in. On the other side of the coin, there was Rocky, a Blue Cochin, who went from a fine boy to a "cockerel from hell" overnight, attacking anyone who went near him and inflicting some pretty awful injuries on me. Sadly, he had to go, because no one wanted to go near him. Most roosters are friendly, become protective of their girls during the breeding season from early spring to late summer, and cause no problems.

A rooster's spurs can become very big, so keep them trimmed. But be careful when you do this; it is easy to make them bleed.

Introducing a cockerel to your flock is usually straightforward, as long as it is mature – aged about one year old is best. If it is too young, it will be bullied by the hens. The only problem you might encounter toward the end of the breeding season is bare patches on the backs of the girls. This is caused by the male treading (mating) his girls. It usually only occurs when a cock has two or three girls. You can spot his favorite because she will be the baldest. Her feathers will regrow in three to five weeks. You can buy saddles on the Internet to protect their skin if it gets too bad. They come in different sizes to accommodate most breeds. If you use them, you will need to check regularly for mites and infections.

A young male chicken is called a cockerel; when he is fully grown (about a year), he is known as a rooster, or cock.

RIGHT: A stunning Brahma cock overlooking his land.

Health and well-being

Anatomy

It is not necessary to know everything about the anatomy of chickens in order to keep them, but it can be useful to have an understanding of how things work so you can recognize early on whether there is a problem or not. It's also useful to know where chickens' ears are – most people do not realize that hens have them. Knowing how chickens eat will enable you to keep an eye on their diet, and realizing what a cecal dropping is can prevent you from panicking for no reason. All of which will hopefully help you relax and enjoy your girls without worrying.

RIGHT: A red sex-link free ranging, looking very happy and healthy.

Combs, Beaks, Eyes, Wattles, and Ears

• **Combs:** There are many types of combs. They are not all red; some are purple. What shape and size they are depends on the breed and sex of the chicken. Roosters tend to have larger combs, which are used to attract females. A comb's main purpose is to help cool the birds in hot weather.

Chickens do not sweat; instead they circulate blood to their combs and wattles, where the body heat radiates and cools the chicken. The seven common comb types are: buttercup, cushion, comb, rose, single, strawberry, and V-shaped.

In very cold weather the chickens can suffer from frostbite. This can be avoided by applying petroleum jelly. (See page 130.)

• **Beaks** are used for picking up food, and should be a natural shape. Trimming the tip of the birds' beaks sometimes occurs in commercially kept birds, as it stops them being able to feather-peck each other.

• **Eyes:** Chickens have very good eyesight and see in color. Their eyes work independently.

• **Wattles** hang below the beak and are usually bigger on the male. They are used to help cool the chickens in hot weather.

• **Ears** are small holes covered by feathers. There is a link between the color of the earlobe and the color of the egg laid. Chickens with white earlobes always lay white eggs. Those with red ones usually lay brown eggs.

ABOVE: The bright eye of a healthy chicken. OPPOSITE TOP LEFT: The comb of a white Silkie cockerel. TOP RIGHT: A normal chicken beak. BOTTOM LEFT: A chicken's ear. BOTTOM RIGHT: The blue skin of a Silkie.

Feathers

OPPOSITE: examples of different feather color patterns. TOP LEFT: Speckled. TOP RIGHT: Buff Laced. BOTTOM LEFT: Penciled, or Partridge. BOTTOM RIGHT: Lemon Mille Fleur.

Feathers repel rain a little, keep chickens warm, and protect their skin from the sun. They also act as a cushion to help protect the body from injuries. There are over three dozen patterns, including: *Barred*, a striped pattern of light and dark alternating horizontally; *Laced*, where the edge of the feather is a different color to the middle; *Spangled*, where there is a teardrop of color on the tip of each feather; *Cuckoo*, where stripes are not as regular and may blend into each other; and *Penciled*, fine dark stripes that follow the shape of the feather — *Silver Penciled* has a silver base color; *Partridge* has a mahogany base.

Chickens either have hard or soft feathers, depending on the breed. Hard feathers grow very close together and cover the body tightly. More fluffy, soft feathers attract many unwanted visitors. (See pages 122–25.) Roosters have different feathers from the hens – they are longer, more pointed, and shinier. Some breeds of chickens even have feathered legs. Birds naturally maintain their own feathers very well and spend a great deal of time preening. They have a gland at the base of their tail that produces oil, which they transfer to the feathers by their beak.

Feathers are molted and replaced annually, usually after the breeding season. It may happen over the entire body all at once or in a specific pattern, starting at the head and neck, followed by the breast and body, and then the wing and tail. It's a stressful time, and your girls may become lethargic. The process takes 8–14 weeks, depending on the breed. During this time egg laying can cease, though it occurs less frequently with hybrids.

WING CLIPPING

Some breeds of chicken are rather good flyers and are capable of flying onto a shed roof. Others are great escape artists. I advise clipping your chickens' wings when you first get them because they can be stressed and nervous when introduced to their new home. You only clip the left wing, as the active ovary makes the bird slightly heavier on this side. This unbalances them, making them less agile and able to fly. If done correctly, it is neither painful nor cruel but is rather like cutting your nails.

You need to cut the first 10 flight (primary, quill) feathers. (See opposite.) Make sure you don't cut any lower than the tip of the other feathers, and never cut the secondary feathers, as the girls use these to keep themselves warm. Wing clipping is a temporary measure because the feathers will regrow. A friend of mine bought some chickens from me, and I clipped her girls' wings for her. She then went home and cut the other (right) wings on all of them because she thought I had forgotten. A week later, I went to visit her and was greeted by her girls getting over her fence and running up to us for biscuits. I couldn't believe it until she sheepishly owned up to what she'd done. We laughed about it because there was nothing we could do, other than raise the fence. The downside of wing clipping is that it does affect the chickens' ability to get away from predators, so only do it if you really have to.

DO ALL CHICKENS NEED WING CLIPPING?

I would recommend that all hybrids , and certainly all White Leghorns, be clipped initially, unless kept in a fully enclosed run.

LEFT: The flight feathers of a chicken's wing before clipping. RIGHT: Clipping the flight feathers.

Legs, spurs, and toes

Chickens' legs are covered in scales, which can be troubled by mites. (See pages 124–26.) Their thighs are covered in feathers. Spurs usually grow only on roosters (sometimes on hens) and they use them to protect themselves and their girls. A rooster's spurs can become very big. Even if he is friendly toward you, keep them trimmed because they can inflict some awful injuries on the hens when he is treading (mating) them. This needs to be done with a good pair of clippers, because the spurs are extremely strong. You just need to take off the sharp tip, not the whole thing, because it will bleed profusely.

Chickens normally have four toes, but some breeds, such as the Silkies, have five. They can injure their toes, but normally they heal quickly with the right treatment. On the end of each toe are nails, which they can lose or break. (See page 130.) Most chickens don't need to have their nails clipped because they are constantly scratching the ground, which keeps them neat. But there are exceptions: light, small breeds sometimes need attention. It is easy to do, but you need to be careful not to clip too much. You can normally see the little blood vessels to avoid. Just take off the tip. If you take off too much, they will bleed a lot, so spray the area with disinfectant and put on a little smear of petroleum jelly. Then keep the chicken separate from the flock so you can keep an eye on her. The bleeding should stop quite quickly.

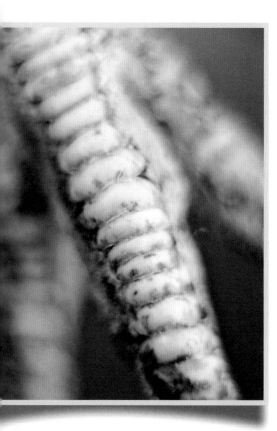

ABOVE: Close-up of
a healthy chicken toe.

How chickens breathe

Chickens have two lungs that are connected to the trachea (windpipe) like us, but that is where the similarities end. Their lungs are fixed to their ribs, so they do not expand. Birds pass air through their lungs using air sacs, which only birds have. Air sacs are small, balloon-like structures that store air inside and act like bellows; this means that the lungs can constantly have air flowing through them. Because chickens depend on the movement of the chest and rib cage to breathe, holding a chicken too tightly can suffocate it.

Chickens have nine air sacs altogether: two surrounding the intestines (abdominal), two at the neck (cervical), one at the shoulder (interclavicular), two beneath the lungs (thoracic anterior), and two behind the lungs (thoracic posterior). Chickens' lungs get fresh air during exhalation (breathing out) and inhalation (breathing in) because it is the air sacs that swell and shrink, and not the lungs. Air flows in through the beak, and half of it goes to the lungs and anterior air sacs. The air from the lungs and anterior sacs then goes out of the mouth, but the air from the posterior air sacs goes back through the lungs. At any time, air can be flowing in and out of the lungs and stored in the air sacs. Chickens also have some hollow bones called pneumatic bones, which aid the respiratory system.

DIGESTIVE SYSTEM

When a chicken eats, its food goes down the esophagus, or gullet. It stops at the crop, where it gets softened. The food then goes through the proventriculus, where the digestive acids are added, and passes down into the gizzard, which has two sets of strong muscles to grind and mash – this is where grit helps. (See page 36.) Then it goes through the intestines, where the nutrients and water are absorbed. Food waste exits through the vent. When a chicken lays an egg, the vagina folds over to let the egg out through the vent, so that it normally doesn't come into contact with any feces.

The crop is an internal pouch at the base of the chicken's neck by the breast and is used to store food and water. You will notice it toward the end of the day as it fills with food. A chicken uses its tongue to push food to the back of its throat, but this doesn't work very well with water, so when it drinks, it tilts its head upward and opens and closes its mouth quickly, which allows the liquid to run into its crop.

Chickens have two blind pouches where the small and large intestines join. These empty a few times a day and produce horrid-smelling feces called cecal droppings. They are usually a mustard color, and they let you know that your chicken's digestive system is working correctly. Normal chicken droppings should be firm and brown with a white cap, which is the urine. Yellow and foamy droppings or those with blood can be a sign of coccidiosis. (See page 128.) White droppings can mean the bird is dehydrated; white runny droppings can be an indication of worms; and green can indicate a severe infestation (or that the bird has eaten too many greens).

General health

Knowing what is normal for your birds is an important part of chicken keeping because spotting signs of illness early can be crucial. In the wild they are prey, and being healthy is necessary for their survival. Chickens are very good at appearing well when you're around; if your girl is exhibiting signs of illness, you can be sure she's been ill for a while. A typical stance of a sick chicken is with its head down, hunched, and looking depressed. If you spot these signs, separating the chicken is imperative; otherwise, she will be pecked and bullied by the others. Separation will also protect the others from whatever is wrong. If another coop is not available, a temporary solution might be to put her in a box indoors with food and water.

I am not a vet, and the remedies I suggest are from my own experience. If you are unsure, call the person from whom you got your birds; they will most likely be happy to help and advise. If symptoms persist and do not respond to treatment, contact a vet – but bear in mind that not all vets deal with chickens regularly enough to warrant a visit. If you obtained your chicken from a good supplier, they will have their own poultry vet and will be happy to give you the phone number. This is another reason why buying from a good supplier is advantageous.

In my experience, natural treatments really do help if administered on a regular basis in the correct amounts. They do not, however, replace wormers, coccidiostats, and veterinary help, and will not make up for inadequate food or water you wouldn't drink yourself, insufficient space, or poor living conditions.

The mention of bird flu makes every chicken keeper freeze with fear. Remember, we hear a lot about it, but it is really confined to poorer parts of Asia where people live in the same room as their chickens. You are very unlikely to encounter it. However, the signs to look for are: their combs and wattles may become blue; the hens will look ill and stand around hunched – and death comes very quickly. It is a notifiable disease. If you have large numbers of birds dying, contact a vet immediately. Some medication prescribed by vets can affect the eggs, so during treatment you should not eat them. A vet will be able to advise you on this.

RIGHT: A group of hybrid hens taking refuge from the rain.

Despite its name, chickens aren't affected by chicken pox – it is solely a human disease.

ABOVE: Lice eggs are normally found at the base of feathers, particularly around the vent.

A-Z OF PARASITES

Flukes

These parasitic worms are leaf-shaped and flat. They may occur along the Eastern shore and near isolated ponds and lakes. Wild birds can introduce them to your chickens, but they rarely cause problems if living conditions are good. They can affect the eyes, skin, and oviduct, causing it to swell and sometimes burst, which will kill the chicken. Symptoms include droopiness, chalky white droppings, and weight loss. Treatment involves keeping your chickens away from ponds, lakes, or boggy land.

Gapeworm

This is a respiratory problem; the adult worm lives in the trachea (windpipe). Symptoms are coughing, gasping, yawning regularly, throwing the head back with the mouth open, shaking of the head, and loss of energy. When you hold your chickens, you'll hear a gurgling sound. If the infestation is severe and left untreated, the birds will suffocate and die. As with all worms (page 127), land rotation is extremely important. The worms' eggs take up to two weeks to hatch. Treatment involves administering an appropriate wormer.

Infectious bronchitis

Otherwise known as IB, this has symptoms similar to those of mycoplasma but, unlike mycoplasma, will infect the whole flock within a few days. Symptoms are coughing and wheezing. If left untreated it can also affect the nervous system, and the chickens will have droopy wings and a twisted neck. In mature hens, droppings may become green, and they may start to lay soft eggs or not lay at all. Most started pullets are vaccinated for IB.

Treatment involves keeping the infected birds warm and looking for any secondary infection that may need antibiotic treatment. Vitamin supplements added to their water helps. There is no known risk to humans.

Lice

These are an external parasite that is species specific, meaning they only like birds. They have a life cycle (egg to mature louse) of approximately three weeks. They spend their entire life on the chickens and will cause great damage to their feathers and their well-being. Signs of a louse infection: the chickens become restless, and scratch and preen continuously; bald patches may appear, particularly around the vent, where the birds will preen away their feathers. Egg production may be affected as the chickens become stressed. If you examine your birds you will see straw-colored lice scurrying around. They can move quickly. They lay their eggs, which are white in color, in clusters at the base of the feathers. (See picture on opposite page.) The eggs will hatch after four to seven days, depending on weather conditions, so treatment should be repeated as necessary.

Treatment is normally done by powdering or spraying the chickens regularly to break the cycle. The lice products are designed just for the animals; there is no need to treat the house because the lice live only on the chicken. Limit wild bird interaction to minimize external parasites.

Mycoplasma gallisepticum

Commonly known as MG, this is a common problem. Being an opportunist organism, it strikes when your birds are under the weather or stressed. The stress trigger can be something as simple as moving them to a new coop, introducing new girls to the flock, or sudden changes in the weather. Symptoms include runny, bubbly eyes, nasal discharge, coughing, sneezing, and in severe cases, swollen eyes.

Wild birds can carry the disease and can easily infect a free-range flock. It is important to make the water and feed as inaccessible to wild birds as possible.

Unfortunately, some chickens do die from this, while some will recover but have similar bouts throughout their lives, and others won't become ill but will be carriers.

Treatment is usually a broad-spectrum antibiotic prescribed only by your vet. I cannot emphasise enough the need to obtain treatment quickly.

If your flock is infected with MG and you choose to cull it and start again, you will need to thoroughly disinfect your coop, feeders, and waterers, and leave them for at least two weeks before introducing new chickens. If possible, move the coop onto fresh ground. *Mycoplasma gallisepticum* poses no risk to humans.

Ticks

If your birds are free range on long grass, ticks might attach themselves. However, this is extremely rare. Removal of the tick needs to be done carefully. If you try to pull them off, the head is often left in the chicken, which will become infected.

Treatment: A quick spray with denatured alcohol will normally make a tick drop off. You can also buy tick removers.

Northern fowl mite

This is probably the worst problem of all because the mite spends its entire life on the chicken, which can do a lot of damage in a short time. You may see the mites crawling both on the chickens' eggs and on the chickens themselves. In severe infestations this causes dark scabs, especially around the vent. I have found that petroleum jelly rubbed over the scabs helps after treatment.

Treating your flock for mites

Natural treatments to deal with mites include Diatom Powder (diatomaceous earth), which is made of micro skeletons of fossilized remains, which have sharp edges that cut the mites' waxy coating, making them dry up and die. It is very effective and available over the Internet in a puffer bottle that works well. It is thought that, when chickens have had garlic, mites don't like the smell that comes off the chicken's skin or the taste of their blood. I crush a clove of garlic and add it to their water regularly. You can also buy garlic granules from pet shops that can be added to the feed. It doesn't make the eggs taste of garlic. Tea tree oil and citronella, which are sold to prevent mosquitoes, and eucalyptus, cedar wood oils, and lemongrass are all said to help repel mites, although I have not tried these.

When using natural remedies, it is usual to use more than one product at a time, change treatment annually, and use varied treatments. You need to break the mites' life cycle, so regular treatments are needed.

Chemical treatments contain the insecticide permethrin, which attacks the mites' nervous system. There is a huge choice of chemical products on the market. Most come in powder form and remain active for some time, but you will need to use them regularly. Place some permethrin powder in a 3×3-foot sandbox, and allow the birds to dust themselves. Some sprays work as a repellent, others by washing the outer wax off the mites, which causes them to dehydrate and die.

Red mite (*Dermanyssus gallinae*)

This is not as big a problem as northern fowl mites, and it is classed as an inconvenience rather than a disaster. How we perceive problems can affect how we deal with them. If you find the mites, don't panic– stay calm and understand what you need to do. Remember red mites do not live on humans; they are host specific, which means that they live and reproduce with the chickens. In severe infestations they may crawl on you, but a shower and change of clothes will remove them. Don't scream, jump around, and cry, because this will not get rid of the critters (I have tried!).

A hysterical lady was once in my yard – she had discovered red mites in her chicken coop. After a chat we soon got the problem into perspective and had a logical action plan drawn up for her to deal with them. She went away with a few products, ready to begin her battle. Two weeks later she had won and now has a very good knowledge of what to look for and what to do next time!

The first part of your plan to deal with them is to understand them and their life cycle. They are external, temporary parasites that live in dark crevices and cracks in the chicken coop, particularly around the ends of perches. They feed on the chickens for between one and two hours at night. They can live for up to eight months with no host to feed on.

The eggs are small, oval, and pearly white. They are laid by the female adult mite in dark cracks and crevices inside the coop and nest box. They usually target the area around the perches first. The eggs will hatch within two to three days in warm weather. Once the eggs hatch, they become larvae, which have six legs and are red in color like an adult mite. At this stage they do not feed on the chickens. They take a day to develop into protonymphs, which have eight legs like an adult mite but are smaller in size. They do, however, start feeding on the chickens, and after about two days they become deutonymphs. These are larger, and after a meal of the chickens' blood, they turn into adult mites. Adult red mites can reproduce and do so rapidly.

Signs to look for are ash-like dust found in cracks; your chickens seeming generally unhappy with a loss of condition; the hens stopping laying; their reluctance to go to bed at night; and spots of blood on their eggs.

One tip is to hang a small, white cloth in the coop at night and check for mites in the morning. Another is to put double-sided tape on the bottom of the perch, which will making spotting them easier and will trap them.

If you catch red mites early, it is much easier and less daunting to deal with than a bad infestation.

BELOW: A group of red mites (*Dermanyssus gallinae*) breeding well in a crevice.

Eliminating red mites from your coop

Insecticide foggers, or bombs, containing permethrin work well because the fogging mist is able to penetrate most crevices. You can also douse the coop with a spray containing permethrin and allow it to dry. The best cure is prevention: see the permethrin powder treatment on page 124.

Breaking the cycle

Whatever method you decide to use, if you have an infestation of northern fowl or red mites, my advice is to use a couple of products to break the cycle, do not stop treatment too early, and routinely dust your chickens and their coop because prevention is better than cure. In order to get the best out of the products you are using, make sure you thoroughly clean the coop of all bedding. If possible, take out any removable parts, such as perches, flooring, and nest boxes. If using sprays, make sure the coop is dry before letting the chickens back in.

Scaly leg mites

Scaly leg mites are a big problem in the U.S. They live on the birds' legs. They are tiny, and burrow under the leg scales – they spend their entire life on the chicken. Treatment needs to be methodical and done thoroughly. Moving the birds onto fresh ground helps. Crusty legs are a sign that your girls are infected.

Treatment involves washing the legs gently and treating them with the appropriate spray, of which there are many on the market. I favor the old-fashioned method of using denatured alcohol on the legs and regularly smothering them in petroleum jelly. Scaly leg mites are very contagious, so don't introduce any new birds into the flock until the problem is resolved.

Worms

Chickens can pick up worms from the land, so land management, or rotation (moving the position of your coop) is very important in order to break the life cycle. Some worms can complete their life cycle with a chicken – i.e., the worm lives in the chicken, which defecates its eggs, which then re-infest the chicken. Some worms need another host – the worm lives in the chicken, which defecates its eggs, which are then eaten by snails/slugs/beetles, earthworms, and the like. The chicken then eats the infected bugs, and the cycle begins again. For backyard homesteaders who raise other species of animals, such as sheep, goats, dogs, and the like, cross contamination is common as well. (This often happens with round and tape worms.) Wild birds can also host worms.

If no chickens are on the land for a while, there is no host for the worms to live in, and so the cycle is broken. You can apply lime to the soil, which helps to deter pests, but removing the birds is the best way to break the cycle. Treatment: wormers are available to buy and easy to use; there are chemical ones and herbal wormers that work by making the inside of the bird uninhabitable. Signs that your birds are suffering from worms include: pale combs, gradual weight loss, generally dull appearance, lethargy, adversely affected laying, and diarrhea.

Farming lore suggests the best time to treat worms is during a full moon, when they are supposed to be at their most active.

A-Z of other health problems

Chickens can get into mischief, and the odd scratch is unavoidable. Any wounds need to be cleaned thoroughly with diluted iodine, then dried and covered with antiseptic spray. You'll need to keep the chicken separate while it heals. The others will almost certainly peck at it. In the summer, watch out for flies. You don't want them bothering the wound. If you notice pus as it heals, draw this out by applying petroleum jelly mixed with garlic. If you are in any doubt, seek help from a vet.

Bumblefoot

This common problem is caused when a cut heals but pus builds up underneath, so check any bird that is limping. Causes can be unsuitable perches; scratching or treading on something sharp; moist litter or muddy runs, which cause the front pad to become chapped and cracked; runs with gravel or weed stubble; and concrete floors without enough litter. You need to catch this early. Treat it by cleaning the foot with warm water and applying iodine. If the skin has healed and pus is still trapped, apply magnesium sulphate paste (available from pharmacies). Sometimes it will need lancing by a vet.

Coccidiosis

This is one of the most common protozoal diseases found in poultry and can occur even in healthy flocks. But cocci are easily controlled by feeding a medicated starter food for the first four to six weeks. This keeps the organisms in check until the birds build a natural immunity.

Dehydration

If a hen goes without water for a couple of days, she may go into a molt and then lay badly for the rest of her life. Signs to watch out for are combs and wattles that are shrivelled and bluish and legs that look bony. Rehydration salts can help if added to the water and are available from pharmacies.

Ear mites

Chickens' ears are commonly affected by mites that go into the ear cavities and start infections – the symptoms will be yellow pus and a horrid smell. The problem is easily dealt with, but advice from a vet is advisable.

Egg bound

A rare condition caused by an egg that is too big to pass. It can also occur in extremely fat hens. Symptoms include frequent visits to the nest box with no eggs being laid; a bird will also seem irritated, and can quickly become

ABOVE: The toes of a chicken. Inspect them regularly for signs of damage.

ill looking and stop eating. If the egg is visible, smear petroleum jelly over the vent to help lubricate it and hold her over a bowl of boiling water so the steam relaxes her muscles, though not so close that you could scald her. If this fails and you can see the egg, carefully make a hole in it and remove all of it with your finger. Any that is left can cause an infection and kill your chicken.

Eye infections

These are often a symptom of an underlying problem, so seek the advice of a vet. If an infection is evident, over-the-counter eye drops can work very well. In any event, clean the eye of pus using cotton wool soaked in cooled boiled salt water at least three times a day, until the infection has cleared and for a few days afterward.

Feather pecking

This usually occurs because of boredom, though sometimes it can be due to lack of protein in a chicken's diet, prolonged hot weather, or stress from bright light or overcrowding. Before jumping to any conclusions, check that loss of feathers isn't because of the molt or because a chicken has lice or mites. If, however, there are V-shape pieces of feather missing, these are beak marks, and your chicken is definitely being feather pecked. Breaking the habit can be a hard job, but it can be done. If the problem is lack of space, either reduce your flock or build a bigger run. Also add toys and distractions. If blood is shed, you need to isolate the victim and deal with her injuries. Once she is healed, you can reintroduce her to the flock. There are anti-peck sprays on the market, which are made to taste and smell unpleasant.

For the offending chicken, you can purchase a plastic bit that makes it impossible for her to close her beak completely but allows her to still eat and drink. These can usually be removed after a couple of weeks. If you have plenty of free time, you can spray the offender with water every time you see her being naughty. Or you can introduce a mature rooster to your flock; he will settle the argument. If you think the problem is being caused by lack of protein, add mealworm or cod liver oil to their feed for a couple of weeks. This is also beneficial because it will help the girls to regrow their feathers.

Frostbite

Chickens are tolerant of cold weather, provided their coop is dry and draft free. Roosters are more likely to suffer than hens because they do not tuck their heads under their wings at night and their combs and wattles are larger. Smearing petroleum jelly on these regularly is a good preventative.

THE CHICKEN MEDICINE CHEST

- Apple cider vinegar
- Iodine
- Rubbing alcohol
- Petroleum jelly
- Garlic
- Cod liver oil
- Mite treatment
- Wormer
- Louse treatment

Gizzard impaction

This happens if birds are fed cut grass, have access to hay, or eat something that can cause an obstruction: the gizzard becomes blocked because it is impacted with fibers. The bird eats, and nothing passes due to the blockage. Because it is hungry, it keeps eating until the crop enlarges and develops a bacterial infection, becoming a sour crop. It can be prevented by feeding the chicken small- to medium-size granite grit. To try to move the blockage, place some olive oil into the bird's mouth and gently massage the crop to loosen and move the impaction. Hang the girl upside down and, with gentle downward movements from the crop to the beak, help her regurgitate the blockage. Only do this for short periods, as she will find it difficult to breathe. If this fails, add a little more olive oil to soften the crop, and wait to see if the impaction moves the other way. If the bird is still unwell and not eating after 24 hours, seek the help of a vet.

Heat stroke

This can adversly affect chickens' appetites and result in interrupted laying or laying fewer or smaller eggs. Chickens cannot sweat but instead pant to cool themselves. Heavy breeds suffer more from heat than lighter breeds. White birds are less susceptible because they reflect heat better than dark birds. During hot weather, providing shade and plenty of cool water is essential. I half-fill bottles with water, freeze them, and then place them in the run. Rehydration salts can also help. Hosing down the outside of their coop can help cool temperatures, and misting adult birds with a fine spray can make them more comfortable.

ABOVE: Feathers worn away by the treading of an amorous rooster. RIGHT: A group of purebred pullets eagerly coming out in the morning.

Internal laying

This is caused by the yolk not dropping into the infundibulum when it is released by the ovaries. As the yolks build up in the bird's abdomen, they are slowly broken down by the body, However, hens that produce a yolk a day cannot deal with the excess yolks, which build up to the point at which they can kill the chicken. The chicken's rear end will lower because of the weight, and she will begin to walk like a penguin. No one knows why this happens and there is no known cure, so humane dispatch will be required.

Lost nails

Chickens occasionally lose their nails. If they do, a good cleaning, followed by an antiseptic spray, is all that is necessary.

Marek's Disease

Marek's is a highly contagious viral disease that affects mainly young birds, for which there is no cure. Infected birds will have paralyzed legs and wings. Silkies and Sebrights are the two most susceptible pure breeds; most hybrids are vaccinated as day-old chicks.

Pasting

Occurs when loose droppings stick to the vent area of chicks. It is thought to be caused by inadequate diet and/or the chick becoming too cold. It does not spread from chick to chick. Once you clear the manure, the condition usually clears up on its own in a few days. But unless you pick the droppings away, the vent may get sealed shut and the chick will die. If it does not clear, you will need to cull the affected chick.

Sour crop

Usually caused by an impacted gizzard ("Gizzard Impaction,"page 130), the first sign of this is an enlarged crop that feels like a balloon part-filled with water. Because the crop cannot empty, it develops its own microflora. Remove the bird. To clear the crop, hang the bird by her legs and gently massage the liquid out. You will need to do this a couple of times, but not for too long because it will be uncomfortable for her. Once the crop is cleared, add probiotic yogurt to her layer's crumbles for a few days; this helps balance the micro-flora in her digestive system. Also disinfect the waterers.

Splayed legs

This happens when chicks are raised on a slippery surface or if the incubator temperature was too high. If a chick hatches with splayed legs, it is possible to *hobble* them using a small strip of to tape to bind their legs into the correct position, though only for a few days. If caught early, this should correct the problem. If it doesn't, the chick will need to be humanely culled.

Sprains and broken legs

A chicken's legs can often suffer from sprains and require rest. Causes include perches that are too high and over-amorous roosters. Overweight birds are also prone to this problem. Broken legs are rare and humane dispatch is the best solution. However, I had a customer who had his hen's leg amputated by a vet because he had accidentally trodden on it himself and broken it. Although she adapted well to her new life, she obviously couldn't scratch around, which is a chicken's favorite pastime, and was kept on her own because the other girls bullied her. In my opinion, it is cruel to keep a chicken on its own because they are flock animals, so when thinking of treatments, please think of the chicken and not yourselves.

Tumors

Tumors are most likely to form internally on the reproductive organs. They are a common cause for poor egg laying. Some tumors are an indication of other problems, such as Marek's Disease, but others are not. Slow-growing tumors in older hens are common, but little is known about them.

Death

Dispatch is a nicer way of saying kill, which makes nearly everyone gasp. Unfortunately it is a part of keeping chickens that you need to know about.

Dispatching a chicken can be done by your vet if you really cannot face it, but if your girl is suffering, making her wait for an appointment and endure the stress of the trip can be unfair. For many years I never had to dispatch any because my husband was always on hand to do the deed. Then he decided that they were my chickens and my responsibility, and he refused to do it again. I was shocked, but as he could never remember my birthday, I thought he wouldn't remember his decision. Months passed, then Gertie, my eight-year-old hen, lost the use of her legs. She was in a sorry state, and there was only one kind thing to do for her. I shouted for my husband, who smiled and said, "Your chickens, your responsibility." Feeling furious but determined, I scooped her up and cuddled her, and took her to a quiet place away from the other girls. There was the log and the axe we'd used for the Christmas turkey (I named the turkey Trevor after my husband to make it easier to dispatch), but I couldn't use it, so with tears running down my cheeks, I dislocated her neck. It was quick and remarkably easy, apart from the emotional side, which I will never find easy. But I'm glad my husband made me do it; otherwise, I never would have.

Cervical dislocation is the most common approved method. It is a quick and easy way of dispatching, as long as you know what you are doing. Never hesitate, and always do it smoothly and quickly. First catch your girl calmly, talk to her, and take her to a quiet place away from the other girls. Then, hold the legs in your left hand if you are right-handed or the right hand if you are left-handed. Using your dominant hand, place the head between your first and second fingers and your thumb under the beak, tilting her head slightly. With a very firm, meaningful, downward action pull the neck and bring the head backward. You should feel a pop as the neck breaks. When you hear this, the job is done. She will flap and kick for a short whole. This is perfectly normal. It is only the reaction of the nervous system.

What can go wrong? If you do not pull down hard and firmly, you will end up stretching the neck and not actually killing her, so if you are going to attempt it, do not hesitate or do it half-heartedly. The worst-case scenario of pulling too hard is that her head will come off, which would be very unpleasant for you — but at least you would know that you did the job thoroughly.

Chopping the head off sounds horrendous but is very effective, and little can go wrong. You need a large, flat log, with two large nails driven into it about 1½ inches apart, and a very sharp axe. Calmly take your girl to an area away from the other girls. Place her head between the nails, and squeeze them together to hold the head in place. In one firm movement chop off the head with the axe.

Throat slitting is best done using a killing cone, which is placed over the chicken's head so that her head pops out of the bottom. You then take a very sharp knife and cut her throat, making sure you cut the jugular vein. She will bleed to death very quickly. This method is favored by small farming organizations that raise chickens for meat.

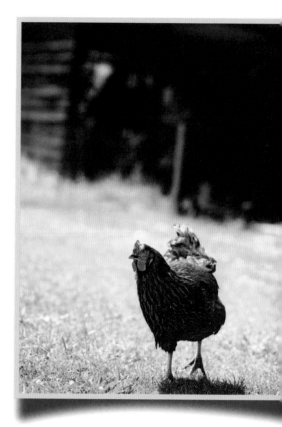

ABOVE: A chicken enjoying an afternoon wander.

Normally chickens live for between six and eight years. The oldest chicken, according to the The Guinness Book of Records, lived until the ripe old age of 16.

Glossary

Air cell the space at the broad end of the egg. Its size indicates the freshness of the egg and, during incubation, the humidity levels.

Bantam miniature breeds, about a quarter the size of normal chickens. See also True bantam.

Barred striped pattern on feathers of light and dark coloring alternating horizontally.

Beak trimming the trimming of the tip of the upper beak to prevent feather pecking.

Beard fluffy feathers under the beak of bearded breeds.

Bedding material laid on the floor of a coop for comfort, insulation, and soaking up feces.

Bloom protective layer deposited on an egg at laying.

Broody the stage in a chicken's reproductive cycle during which it incubates eggs.

Bumblefoot swelling and infection of the foot pad.

Candling a method for seeing inside an egg by holding it up to a beam of light to illuminate its contents.

Capon a castrated male chicken used for meat.

Chick crumble chicken feed with a high protein content designed for chicks aged 0–6/8 weeks.

Clipping cutting through the 10 flight feathers of a single wing to stop the bird from flying.

Cloaca another term for a chicken's bottom. *See also* Vent.

Cock a male chicken older than 12 months. See also Rooster.

Cockerel male chicken younger than 12 months.

Comb the red membrane on a chicken's head. It is a cooling mechanism for chickens.

Coop a pen or cage for containing poultry.

Crest the display of feathers on top of a chicken's head in crested breeds like the Polish.

Crop the internal pouch at the base of a chicken's neck in front of the wishbone. The sac stores food until it is released into the digestive tract.

Crumbles ready-prepared feed that is suitable for chickens laying eggs.

Cuckoo stripes on feathers, stripes that are not regular and may blend into each other.

Culling the humane killing of ill or unwanted birds.

Down soft, fluffy feathers, typical of chicks.

Dust bath a clean, dry area of soil or sand where birds "bathe."

Egg tooth the small horn on the tip of a chick's beak. It is designed to help the chick break out of the egg. Within 48 hours it dries and falls off.

Feeder the container in which feed is placed.

Frizzle feathers that curl backwards, giving a "permed" appearance.

Gizzard the muscular pouch within the bird's digestive system, which helps grind their food using grit.

Grit tiny bits of stone for grinding food in the gizzard.

Grit station the container in which grit is placed.

Grower's crumbles or pellets ready-prepared feed that is suitable for growing chickens aged 6/8–16 weeks.

Hackle the feathered area at the back of the neck.

Harden off to gradually take away an artificial heat

source from newly hatched chicks.

Hen a female chicken over 1 year old, normally past its first annual molt.

Hopper another term for a feeder.

Hybrid a bird whose parentage comes from two distinctly different breeds.

In lay the term used to describe a chicken that's laying eggs.

Laced where the edge of the feathers is a different color to the middle.

Layer a chicken that is producing eggs.

Mash ready-prepared chicken feed that is similar to crumbles or pellets but in milled form.

Molt the method by which birds replace their feathers once a year.

Muff the feathers on a chicken's cheeks, attached to the beard.

Nest box the box in which hens lay. It should be positioned somewhere quiet and secluded.

Pecking order the order of dominance by which chickens arrange themselves.

Pellets ready-prepared chicken feed in bite-sized pieces that is usually a complete diet ration.

Penciled very fine stripes that follow the shape of the feather, resulting in two areas of dark color.

Perch a rod or bar on which hens sleep above the ground, as though in a tree.

Pipping the way a chick breaks into the air cell and then through the cell in its egg before hatching.

Plumage a bird's complete coat of feathers.

Pop hole entrance into a coop or run, usually closed by a door or sliding shutter.

Poultry saddle a cloth placed on the back of a chicken to protect her from the male's spurs and claws or from feather pecking.

Preening the way in which a bird cleans and arranges its feathers.

Pullet a female chicken under 1 year old.

Pure breed hens that hatch male and female chicks that share common characteristics and always breed true.

Rooster a male chicken older then 12 months. See also Cock.

Saddle the back area of a chicken, around the hips.

Scales the overlapping plates protecting the skin on a chicken's legs.

Sex-linked an inherited trait, like color, linked to the sex of either parent. Useful in identifying the sex of very young birds.

Spangled feathers with a dark teardrop-shape of color on the tip of each feather.

Spur the horny growth on the rear of a male's legs.

Started pullet the stage of a female chicken's life at which it can start to lay eggs. It can occur at any time between 16–24 weeks.

Treading an alternative term for mating.

True bantam a breed about a quarter the size of normal chickens but which has no large equivalent.

Vent a chicken's bottom. There is no vaginal opening in birds, so their eggs are laid through the same one though which they excrete.

Waterer the container in which water is placed.

Wattle the flesh hanging from the face by the beak. It is often red, like the comb, and helps in cooling the chicken.

Index

Index

Resources

Coops, Runs, Tractors, Fencing

Chicken Coop Mart
Includes kits
888-286-2347, ext. 722
chickencoopmart.com

Chicken Coop Select
Includes kits
848-228-3857
chickencoopselect.com

Chicken Coop Source
Includes kits
866-749-9504
chickencoopsource.com

EZ Clean Coops
Upscale coops
888-743-8026
ezcleancoops.com

Horizon Structures
Includes kits
888-447-4337
horizonstructures.com

Williams-Sonoma
Yes, that Williams –Sonoma!
877-812-6235
williams-sonoma.com

Feed

GMO Free Idaho
Specializes in non-GMO feed
gmofreeidaho.com

H and H Old-Fashioned Chicken Feed
Soy-free, non-GMO, fresh milled feed
512-755-2512
handhsoyfreechickenfeed.com

Modesto Milling Organic Feed
Certified organic feed
800-897-9740
modestomilling.com

Scratch and Peck Feeds
Soy-free and non-GMO feed
360-318-7585
scratchandpeck.com

Feeders, Waterers, Wormers, Equipment

The Chicken Hutch
Includes coops and fencing
310-832-9981
thechickenhutch.com

Fleming Outdoors
Includes coops and fencing
800-642-4493
flemingoutdoors.com

Harris Farms
harrisfarmsllc.com

Kuhl Corporation
908-782-5696
kuhlcorp.com

Stromberg's Chicks & Game Birds Unlimited
Includes feed, coops, fencing
800-720-1134
strombergschickens.com

Verm-X
Parasite control in liquid and pellet forms, plus nutritional supplements; certified organic
866-942-0042
verm-xusa.com

Hatcheries

Belt Hatchery
Fresno, CA
559-264-2090
belthatchery.com

Cackle Hatchery
Lebanon, MO
417-532-4581
cacklehatchery.com

Central Hatchery
Madison, NE
800-272-2449

Clearview Stock Farm and Hatchery
Gratz, PA
717-365-3234

DarkEggs.com
McConnells, SC
877-572-8266
darkeggs.com

Ideal Poultry Breeding Farms
Cameron, TX
254-697-6677
ideal-poultry.com

Sand Hill Preservation Center
Calamus, IA
563-246-2299
sandhillpreservation.com

Shady Lane Poultry Farm
Columbus, IN
812-603-7722
shadylanepoultry.com

Shook Poultry
Claremont, NC
828-459-0571
shookpoultry.net

Information

Backyard Poultry Magazine
800-551-5691
backyardpoultrymag.com

Educational resources
extension.psu.edu/animals/poultry/topics

General resource site
extension.psu.edu/animals/poultry

Hobby Farms; Hobby Farm Home; Urban Farm
Magazines of interest to backyard homesteaders
800-627-6157
hobbyfarmsmagazine.com

Poultry Press
Monthly newspaper since 1914
765-827-0932
poultrypress.com

Urban-specific chicken info
extension.psu.edu/animals/poultry/topics/urban-and-small-poultry-production

Organizations

American Bantam Association
bantamclub.com

American Pastured Poultry Producers Association
570-584-2309
apppa.org

American Poultry Association
724-729-3459
ampltya.com

Acknowledgments

Special thanks to all my friends for their help and support: Amanda, Ian, Roy, and Judy for their celebrating in style! Ben and Cathie for just being them, absolute rocks. Ed, who manages to put up with me most days. Will for his humor and honest insults! Luke for all his knowledge and support when things go wrong. Everyone at Kyle Books who has made this possible. Lastly, my four children and husband for their constant help and enthusiasm, even in the snow, and their love.

Dedication
To Mom and Dad, for my fantastic childhood and where it has led!

First published in North America in 2013 by

CREATIVE
HOMEOWNER®

Creative Homeowner® is a registered trademark of Federal Marketing Corporation

Chickens for the Backyard Homesteader

Library of Congress Control Number: 2012949103
ISBN-13: 978-1-58011-713-5   ISBN-10: 1-58011-713-9

Current Printing (last digit): 10 9 8 7 6 5 4 3 2 1

First published in Great Britain in 2012 by Kyle Books,
An imprint of Kyle Cathie, 23 Howland Street, London, W1T 4AY
general.enquiries@kylebooks.com   www.kylebooks.com

Text © 2012 Suzie Baldwin; Photographs © 2012 Cristian Barnett ;
Illustrations © 2012 Becca Thorne; Design © 2012 Kyle Books

Technical consultant: Pillip J. Clauer, Senior Instructor, Pennsylvania State University,
**   Department of Animal Science, Specialty Poultry**
Editor: Judith Hannam
Editorial assistant: Laura Foster
Designer: Laura Woussen
Photographer: Cristian Barnett
Illustrator: Becca Thorne
Copy editor: Liz Murray
Proofreader: Catherine Ward
Production: Lisa Pinnell

Color reproduction by Scanhouse
Printed and bound in China

CREATIVE HOMEOWNER, A Division of Federal Marketing Corporation
24 Park Way, Upper Saddle River, NJ 07458

www.creativehomeowner.com

METRIC EQUIVALENTS

Length

1 inch	25.4mm
1 foot	0.3048m
1 yard	0.9144m
1 mile	1.61km

Area

1 square inch	645mm²
1 square foot	0.0929m²
1 square yard	0.8361m²
1 acre	4046.86m²
1 square mile	2.59km²

Volume

1 cubic inch	16.3870cm³
1 cubic foot	0.03m³
1 cubic yard	0.77m³

Capacity

1 fluid ounce	29.57mL
1 pint	473.18mL
1 quart	0.95L
1 gallon	3.79L

Weight

1 ounce	28.35g
1 pound	0.45kg

Temperature

Fahrenheit = Celsius x 1.8 + 32
Celsius = Fahrenheit - 32 x ⅝